the About.com guide to
QUILTING

From Pattern to Patchwork—
Creative Projects You Can Finish in Under a Week

Janet Wickell

Adams Media
Avon, Massachusetts

About About.com

About.com is a powerful network of 600 Guides—smart, passionate, accomplished people who are experts in their fields. About.com Guides live and work in more than twenty countries and celebrate their interests in thousands of topics. They have written books, appeared on national television programs, and won many awards in their fields. Guides are selected for their ability to provide the most interesting information for users, and for their passion for their subject and the Web. The selection process is rigorous—only 2 percent of those who apply actually become Guides. The following are some of the most important criteria by which they are chosen:

- High level of knowledge/passion for their topic
- Appropriate credentials
- Keen understanding of the Web experience
- Commitment to creating informative, actionable features

Each month more than 48 million people visit About.com. Whether you need home-repair and decorating ideas, recipes, movie trailers, or car-buying tips, About.com Guides can offer practical advice and solutions for everyday life. Wherever you land on About.com, you'll always find content that is relevant to your interests. If you're looking for "how to" advice on refinishing your deck, About.com will also show you the tools you need to get the job done. No matter where you are on About.com, or how you got here, you'll always find exactly what you're looking for!

About Your Guide

 Janet Wickell began quilting during the quilt revival of the 1970s and it didn't take long for her to become hooked on the craft. In the 1990s she collaborated with her sister Donna to write *Quick Little Quilts*, a book that shows readers how to make easy and accurate miniature quilts and wall hangings. She also authored *Easy-to-Make Dollhouse Quilts*, a collection of foundation pieced quilts made from 1" blocks, and *Teach Yourself Quilting*, a complete reference for beginning to experienced quilters.

Janet was the freelance writer for numerous books in Rodale Press's Classic American Quilt Collection series and she has contributed to many other quilting books and patterns for major publishers. She has taught quilting and hand marbling at the John C. Campbell Folk School in Brasstown, North Carolina.

Janet has been an About.com Guide since 1999, and she wrote its Home Buying and Selling Web site for several years. She is co-owner of a real estate agency and fudge shop in North Carolina.

Acknowledgments

I would like to say a big "Thank You!" to all of the people who made this book possible. That list includes the staff at About .com and Adams Media, and my family and co-workers—who always understand when I disappear for weeks on end to write. And especially to the members of the About.com Quilting community, who inspire me every day. Some of our forum hostesses were kind enough to test patterns and make quilts for this book. You'll see a preview of their wonderful work in the color insert. Thank you all.

ABOUT.COM

CEO & President
Scott Meyer

COO
Andrew Pancer

SVP Content
Michael Daecher

Director, About Operations
Chris Murphy

Senior Web Designer
Jason Napolitano

ADAMS MEDIA

Editorial

Publishing Director
Gary M. Krebs

Managing Editor
Laura M. Daly

Acquisitions Editor
Brielle K. Matson

Development Editor
Katrina Schroeder

Marketing

Director of Marketing
Karen Cooper

Assistant Art Director
Frank Rivera

Production

Director of Manufacturing
Susan Beale

Production Project Manager
Michelle Roy Kelly

Senior Book Designer
Colleen Cunningham

About.com® is a registered trademark of About, Inc.
Published by Adams Media, an F+W Publications Company
57 Littlefield Street, Avon, MA 02322
www.adamsmedia.com

ISBN-10: 1-59869-344-1
ISBN-13: 978-1-59869-344-7

Printed in China.
J I H G F E D C B A

Library of Congress Cataloging-in-Publication Data
Wickell, Janet.
The About.com guide to quilting / Janet Wickell.
p.   cm. — (An about.com series book)
ISBN-13: 978-1-59869-344-7 (flexibound)
ISBN-10: 1-59869-344-1 (flexibound)
1. Quilting. 2. Patchwork. 3. Appliqué. I. Title.
TT835.W5 2007
746.46'0410285—dc22   2007008141

This publication is designed to provide accurate and authoritative information with regard to the subject matter covered. It is sold with the understanding that the publisher is not engaged in rendering legal, accounting, or other professional advice. If legal advice or other expert assistance is required, the services of a competent professional person should be sought.
        —From a *Declaration of Principles* jointly adopted by a Committee of the American Bar Association and a Committee of Publishers and Associations

Many of the designations used by manufacturers and sellers to distinguish their product are claimed as trademarks. Where those designations appear in this book and Adams Media was aware of a trademark claim, the designations have been printed with initial capital letters.

Interior photographs taken by Elisabeth Verde.

This book is available at quantity discounts for bulk purchases. For information, please call 1-800-289-0963.

How to Use This Book

Each About.com book is written by an About.com Guide—an expert with experiential knowledge of his or her subject. While the book can stand on its own as a helpful resource, it can also be coupled with the corresponding About.com site for even more tips, tools, and advice. Each book will not only refer you back to About.com, but it will also direct you to other useful Internet locations and print resources.

All About.com books include a special section at the end of each chapter called Get Linked. Here you'll find a few links back to the About.com site for even more great information on the topics discussed in that chapter. Depending on the topic, you could find links to such resources as photos, sheet music, quizzes, recipes, or product reviews.

About.com books also include four types of sidebars:

- **Ask Your Guide:** Detailed information in a question-and-answer format
- **Tools You Need:** Advice about researching, purchasing, and using a variety of tools for your projects
- **What's Hot:** All you need to know about the hottest trends and tips out there
- **Elsewhere on the Web:** References to other useful Internet locations

Each About.com book will take you on a personal tour of a certain topic, give you reliable advice, and leave you with the knowledge you need to achieve your goals.

CONTENTS

CONTENTS . . . *continued*

Introduction from Your Guide

There's never been a better time to be a quilter. We have hundreds of years of quilting history to draw from for inspiration, but the advancements made in the craft since the 1970s far surpass all of the developments that occurred prior to that time. Today's quilters have a huge array of tools and fabrics to draw from when they create their quilts. Manufacturers work hard to develop products especially for us, from sewing machines that can mimic hand quilting and produce incredible embroidery to all of the small tools we need to complete every step of the quiltmaking process.

None of the recent advancements indicate that we've forgotten our quilting heritage—far from it. Walk into any quilt shop and explore fabrics stores online and you'll find books and magazines filled with historical information and traditional patterns. Quilting fabric manufacturers are producing more and more reproductions of vintage fabrics that let us recreate quilting styles from any era. Thread makers have joined in to give us vintage colors to sew with.

A growing number of quilters have become interested in art quilts during the past decade. You'll see self portraits, landscapes, optical illusions, and all sorts of freeform designs—there's no end to the subjects that can be translated to cloth to create a quilt. Stitch whatever moves you, because making an art quilt is all about the freedom of expressing yourself in cloth.

Even though we can choose to spend thousands and thousands of dollars to purchase special quilting equipment, it isn't necessary. Any sewing machine that sews a straight line is all you need to assemble your quilts quickly, and who knows, you might decide you would rather sew every patch together by hand. As you work through this book you'll find that some tools are must haves, while others are optional or can be replaced with items you might already own.

There is one thing I'd like you to take away from this book: there are no rules. Yes, there are lots of guidelines that will help you learn to make your first quilts, and I've tried to cover the most important instructions, but making a quilt is all about choices. Get the basics behind you, and then listen to your own gut instincts when it's time to sew. Alter a sewing method if doing so makes it work better for you. If you make a mistake, move on—mistakes are wonderful learning experiences. New quilting tools and techniques are developed by quilters just like you—people who saw a need for a product or a better way of doing something and set out to develop it.

I hope you'll try all of the patterns in this book, but branch out a bit with each one if you feel comfortable making changes. Use your own favorite fabric styles and colors instead of the ones I've chosen. Refer to the general instructions to learn how to add more borders, or borders of different widths. Make the quilt larger or smaller. Change a quilt's setting. Those alterations might seem insignificant, but they're the first steps toward designing your own quilts.

Plan to visit us online, at http://quilting.about.com, and join our growing quilting community. You'll find a Web site filled with articles and patterns, and three quilting forums where you can share quilting ideas and talk about life in general with other quilters. You'll discover that quilters are among the most thoughtful, giving groups of people around. They love to teach and they'll welcome you to the group with open arms.

Chapter 1

Quilting Basics

What Is a Quilt?

Throughout history a high percentage of quilts that were made were purely utilitarian, constructed to provide warm bed coverings. More intricate quilts were used as decorative objects and were often given as gifts. Extreme care went into the creation of quilts that the maker hoped would be heirloom items passed down through the generations. Quilters probably didn't realize that even their very basic pieces would become instant heirlooms a century later when discovered by someone who appreciates the time and care that were used to make them.

Described in the simplest terms, a quilt is a textile object made by combining three layers of materials and then holding those layers together with some sort of stitches. The top layer of a quilt is usually the most decorative layer. The middle layer is made from a filler material of some type, usually a thick product called **batting** that can be made from natural or synthetic fibers. The reverse layer of the quilt is called the **backing**, and while it's most often

About

▶ Redwork quilts were popular early in the twentieth century and we've seen renewed interest in them recently. Redwork quilts feature embroidered quilt blocks and got their name from the colorfast Turkey red thread that crafters used to make them. Additional colors of embroidery threads were used as colorfast versions became available. You'll see pictures of many vintage Redwork quilts online, including a quilt made in about 1915 that is part of the quilt collection at the Illinois State Museum. Visit www.quiltindex.org and do a quick search for redwork friendship.

made from a simple panel of fabric, the backing can be decorative in its own right. The act of sewing these three layers together is called quilting (not to be confused with quiltmaking, the general act of making a quilt).

Most quilts fall into one of three very basic categories: **patchwork**, **appliqué**, and **whole cloth**—names that describe how a quilt is constructed. Those designations sound simple until you explore the many variations within each group. Let's talk about commonly used terms to help you recognize and classify a few different types of quilts.

Patchwork Quilts

Patchwork quilts are the most popular type of quilt. Also called pieced quilts, they are made by cutting fabric patches of varying shapes and sizes and sewing the pieces together to create a design. The quilter typically assembles small patchwork units, called quilt blocks, and sews them together in rows to create the top layer of a quilt. Some types of patchwork quilts are all-over designs that do not have individual blocks.

The projects in this book all contain patchwork, and you'll read about several types of patchwork techniques in the general quilting chapters. The foundation-pieced quilts you'll read about in Chapter 8 fall into the patchwork category, even though fabrics are sewn to an underlying base in order to follow a pattern or keep them stable.

Like other quilting techniques, patchwork can be done by hand or machine. Strip piecing and other quick-piecing methods found in Chapter 7 describe how to assemble and then cut large components into the smaller pieces required for a patchwork quilt. Quick piecing eliminates the handling of small pieces of fabric, and removing that task helps you make accurate patchwork quilts.

Appliqué Quilts

Appliqué quilts are made by sewing smaller pieces of fabric on top of a larger background. Like a patchwork quilt, an appliqué quilt can be made up of individual blocks that are sewn together. Quilt designs are varied, so you'll find that other appliqué quilts are made by arranging and sewing motifs to a large piece of cloth instead.

Traditional appliqué quilts are assembled by turning patch edges under as you hand sew each piece to the background. That technique is still popular, but in Chapter 5 you'll learn several additional methods to help you construct hand- and machine-sewn appliqué quilts.

Album quilts were inspired by the autograph books and scrapbooks kept by women during the nineteenth century—much like the scrapbooks that are kept today. Album quilts can be made using any technique, but the most intricate versions of vintage quilts were created with appliqué. Each block in a traditional album quilt was made by a different quilter. The finished quilts were assembled and given as gifts for special occasions, often as wedding presents or as a remembrance when friends and family moved away. Quilt blocks were usually signed with the name of their makers and often included either a quotation or a verse that was significant to the recipient.

Baltimore Album quilts are elaborate versions of album quilts that originated in Baltimore, Maryland, in the mid 1800s. The quilts are made from appliquéd blocks filled with numerous fabrics and intricate designs. Motifs were often stacked or embellished to create three-dimensional flowers and other effects. Baltimore Album quilts are among the many vintage quilt styles that are being interpreted and recreated by today's quilters.

Hawaiian quilting is another special type of appliqué. Quilting as we know it was brought to the Hawaiian Islands by missionaries in the nineteenth century. The islanders liked the technique but soon developed their own unique way of interpreting it. Hawaiian

ELSEWHERE ON THE WEB

▶ The Maryland Historical Society offers an online tour of vintage Baltimore Album quilts, along with historical facts about the quiltmakers. Visit www.mdhs.org/quiltprj/quilthom.html.

appliqué quilts often feature motifs that are found in island surroundings, such as the local vegetation. Other designs are of items important to the culture and history of the region. The appliqué designs are created by folding fabric before cutting it—similar to the way we learned to cut snowflakes from paper when were children. The large, intricate motifs are then sewn to a background fabric.

Whole-Cloth Quilts

Whole-cloth quilts do not contain appliqué or decorative patchwork. Whole-cloth quilts are sewn from a large piece of cloth or from narrower panels of the same fabric sewn together to widen the quilt. The whole-cloth quilts you have seen might have been made from panels of white or another solid color, but printed fabrics are also used to construct them.

A whole-cloth quilt made from a single printed fabric showcases the fabric. Quilting stitches often surround designs within the print to make the designs even more obvious. However, it is the quilting that is the focal point of a solid color, whole-cloth quilt, offering a place for talented quilters to display their machine- or hand-quilting skills.

Trapunto quilts are a special type of whole-cloth quilt. In a trapunto quilt, at least a portion of the spaces between quilting stitches are filled with extra batting to create raised designs. Those areas often depict flowers, leaves, and vines, but any type of motif can be formed.

Traditional hand-quilted trapunto projects are made by assembling the quilt layers and quilting around the areas that will be stuffed with extra batting. After quilting, the quiltmaker turns the quilt over and cuts small slits in the backing fabric, between the quilting lines, and then stuffs cording or batting through the slits. The openings are stitched closed and a second backing is added

▶ You might hear the term cheater cloth, or cheater quilt, when you talk with other quilters. The term refers to preprinted panels that mimic an entire quilt or wall hanging. You can layer preprinted cloth with batting and backing and quilt around the printed patches to make a quick quilt. A variety of panels are usually available at quilt shops. Vintage feedsacks were often printed like this to resemble an entire quilt.

to cover the seams. More quilting stitches are used to secure the layers.

An alternate method uses a loosely woven backing fabric—cloth with threads that can be coaxed apart far enough to insert the stuffing, then eased back together again when the task is complete.

Art Quilts

Beginning quilters are sometimes intimidated by the term art quilt. There's no need to be, because anyone can make an art quilt. There are no rules—an art quilt is the product of your own imagination and can be made using any combination of techniques that you desire.

Art quilts offer an opportunity for individual expression. Fabric can be cut and sewn freeform, or precisely cut patches can be sewn together in a regimented manner. You can use threads, dyes, inks, lace, ribbon, and other products to embellish and add detail to the quilt.

One fun and easy way to get started with art quilts is to make fabric postcards or letter-sized quilts. These small quilts go together quickly and are perfect for trying out new techniques. Committing to using a brand new method is much easier when you know you'll only have to try it out within a 4" x 6" or 8½" x 11" area! If you don't enjoy the method, no problem! You'll be finished with the little quilt in no time. If you want to do more, try the method in more little quilts or incorporate it in your next large quilt. For instructions on how to create a fabric postcard, see Chapter 10. There are also templates in Appendix C.

Landscape quilts are one type of art quilt. Landscape quilts can depict anything you want to recreate on cloth. We see intricately appliquéd landscape quilts, pieced versions, and quilts with

ELSEWHERE ON THE WEB

▶ For machine trapunto, extra batting is used to raise specific areas of the quilt. Designs are outline quilted with water-soluble thread. The second layer of batting is trimmed away from the quilted edges, and then the quilt is sandwiched and quilted as usual. When the quilt is washed the water-soluble stitches disappear, leaving the raised motifs surrounded by permanent quilting stitches. Advanced Embroidery Designs (www.advanced-embroidery-designs.com/projects2/guide_trapunto.html) explains how to use machine embroidery for the technique, but any machine quilted stitches can be used.

▶ Art quilts are often made from a combination of methods and are sometimes embellished with inks and paints. Netting and tulle are often placed over a fabric to either tone it down or add sparkle. Angelina fibers bond together when heat is applied to them, forming sheets of loosely woven color that can be applied to your quilts. There are no limits to the type of materials you can add to an art quilt, so get creative and keep watch for items that suit your theme perfectly.

fabric elements that are cut freehand and sewn to the fabric without finishing the raw edges of the fabric.

The About.com quilting photo galleries contain landscapes of all kinds, from the deserts in the southwestern United States to large floral ink-painted drawings of tropical flowers. You'll find a link to our galleries at the end of this chapter.

Important Quilting Tools

It's easier to sort out the tools you'll need when they're placed into a few basic categories: the main tools you need to get started, the tools you need for specific tasks, and the tools you might want to add to your collection over time. The lists in this chapter mention tools that are useful for many basic quilting tasks. You'll find recommendations for specialty tools within each technique and pattern chapter.

Here's a list of quilting tools that will get you started with most techniques. We'll split the tools into categories, labeling them by the type of work they do and the technique they are used to accomplish. That should help you eliminate tools that are for quilting methods you aren't interested in trying yet. You'll learn more about each of these tools throughout the book within general instructions and quilt pattern chapters.

Basic Multipurpose Quilting Tools

- A seam ripper to remove those little mistakes we always make. Be sure to buy a seam ripper with a small blade that will fit easily under stitches.
- Long straight pins with large, visible heads that you can easily see when they're pinned to fabrics. Pins with yellow heads are one option. Another good choice is Clover straight pins, with flat heads that resemble flowers.

- An iron and ironing board. Choose a heavy iron and let the combination of weight and heat press your fabrics. Any ironing board will do. Plain cotton board covers are my favorites because fabric grips to them slightly and they don't overheat.
- Number 3 or 4 hard lead pencils and sharpener, or a mechanical pencil, for various marking tasks.
- White or yellow marking pencils to mark lines on dark fabrics.
- Chalk or soapstone markers to draw quilting lines.
- Thin cardboard or plastic template material for the occasional pattern that's best to cut with templates.
- A color value filter to help you decide how light and dark fabrics are in relation to each other.

You'll need a few important cutting tools. Because quilting involves a lot of cutting, you'll definitely want to invest in the tools that will make your job easier. Be sure to read the tips in Chapter 6 before you buy rotary cutting tools. If your paper and fabric scissors look alike, label them to avoid dulling fabric blades by accidentally using them for other tasks.

- Rotary cutter and rotary mat
- 6" × 24" rotary ruler
- 12½" × 12½" rotary ruler
- Sharp fabric scissors
- Appliqué scissors with pointed tips
- Paper scissors

Consider a few tools to make machine sewing easier. The big-ticket item in this category is your sewing machine, but it needn't

ASK YOUR GUIDE

I'm not ready to buy all of the tools on the lists. How can I decide which tools I really need?

▶ Read through the patterns in this book and others, and then browse patterns in magazines and on the Internet. Which tools are mentioned most often in the instructions for the patterns that you like the best? Those are the tools to start with. I suggest that you add specialty quilting tools after you have a better feel for the techniques being used or when you decide to try new methods.

be an elaborate model that performs lots of special stitches. Any machine that sews a straight stitch will work just fine. If you already own a sewing machine, use it until you have a better feel for the type of projects you like best, then purchase a new machine that has the options you need to make your quilts.

Several manufacturers make sewing machines especially for quilters, focusing on machine-quilting options and accessories that help us sew accurate seams. Many of today's sewing machines take fancy stitches to a new level with built-in or add-on embroidery units—and the units do a lot more than embroider. You can make lace, sew preformatted quilting motifs, and even cross-stitch.

- Sewing machine and its tool kit
- A brush to remove lint from bobbin area
- Universal sewing machine needles
- Specialty needles: embroidery, denim, machine quilting

Here are some threads you'll need when you make a quilt. Most quilters use all-cotton fabrics to piece the majority of their quilts, and the best match for those fabrics is 100 percent cotton thread. Save your polyester thread for other tasks because it's stronger than cotton fibers and over time will cut through cotton fabric along pieced seams. Thread made by wrapping cotton fibers around a polyester core will do the same. Don't take a chance— buy quality cotton threads for all of your piecing tasks.

- Cotton sewing thread for machine and hand piecing
- Cotton quilting thread for hand quilting
- Decorative threads for quilting and appliqué
- Thin, flat, colorful materials that feed through your needle like thread

Quilters use many types of decorative threads to quilt and embellish their projects after they are pieced. Keep in mind that those threads could cut through fabric over time. Consider how the quilt will be used when you choose specialty threads and stick to cotton for quilts that will actually be used and washed, because use will shift threads and put stress on fabrics. Save the decorative threads for wall quilts and other projects that won't be put through much wear and tear.

There are specific tools you'll need to piece your quilts by hand. Hand piecing is a technique that more and more quilters are turning to as a quiet way to unwind after a busy day. There's something very personal about a quilt that you sew entirely by hand. Every little stitch is an important link in the chain of threads that hold patches together.

- Hand-sewing needles: sharps or milliners
- Cotton sewing threads
- Template-making materials
- Marking pencils
- Thimble, if desired

Following are some tools you need to finish the quilt. Finishing techniques differ, but there are a few universal tools that will help you complete the quilt. Read finishing details in Chapter 9 to learn how some of these tools are used.

- Darning needles for basting and tying
- Stainless steel safety pins for pin basting
- Walking foot for straight-line machine quilting
- Darning or quilting foot for free-motion machine quilting
- Betweens, needles for hand quilting
- Machine-quilting or embroidery needles

ELSEWHERE ON THE WEB

▶ One of my favorite thread companies is YLI. Pay a visit to the company's Web site if you're ready to be inspired by a huge assortment of hand- and machine-sewing threads and a variety of ribbons for embellishment. YLI offers free instructions for patterns and techniques and maintains a special page that describes its new products. Visit www.ylicorp.com.

Online Quilting Community

Some quilters still get together in person to assemble and quilt their projects, especially quilters in church groups or those who belong to quilting guilds. Guilds are clubs that typically meet once a month to have fun and sponsor educational events. They often hold an annual quilt show to display their work to other quilters and members of their communities.

Today, all quilters have the opportunity to belong to a group, even if they don't have a local club to join. The Internet makes it possible for quilters from all over the world to meet each other and share their love of quilting online. It's easy to join in the conversations taking place in quilting forums, special destinations where you can send a message for all forum members to read and respond to.

Quilting groups are located all over the Web. If you're having a problem with a technique, post a question online and someone will have an answer for you. If you want to share a tip, post that too; someone will be grateful for the advice. Most forum messages are organized into folders—sort of like an online filing cabinet. Each folder is labeled with a specific topic. Just choose the topic that suits your question or comment and add your message.

You can join fabric and quilt block swaps online. Quilters definitely enjoy meeting and talking with other quilters online, but some of the most active folders in the About.com Quilting site forums are the folders set up for fabric and quilt block swaps. Each swap is managed by one of our hosts or hostesses, quilters who have participated in our swaps several times and know how to develop a swap that will be fun for all participants.

Joining fabric swaps is a good way for beginners to get started in our community. In a fabric swap, you'll typically buy one fabric and cut it into smaller pieces. The pieces are sent to a central location or directly to other swappers. You receive a piece of fabric

▶ We have three forums at the Quilting site on About .com. The Quilting Forum is where you'll find all sorts of quilt talk, from general quilting questions to specific techniques, even fabric swaps. The Art Quilts Forum is a special place to talk about art quilts and all of the special techniques used to create them. The Quilting Professionals' Forum is a place where quilt pros can tell you about their quilting products and services. It's also a forum where members can talk about the ups and downs of running a quilt-related business. Visit http://about.com/quilting/forum.

back for each one you send, and the pieces you receive are nearly always a nice variety of fabrics. Swaps are a wonderful way to accumulate lots of different fabrics in a short time.

Centralized and decentralized swaps are different. You'll see the terms centralized and decentralized when you read guidelines for quilting swaps. In a centralized swap, all items are sent to the person hosting the swap. That person sorts the items and sends full swap packets back to everyone at one time. If you send ten pieces of fabric, you'll get ten pieces back.

If you join a decentralized swap it means you will send items to each individual swapper, and they'll do the same for you. Packets are typically received over a period that extends from a few weeks to a month, depending on when each quilter puts items in the mail and how far they must travel to get to you.

There are pros and cons to each type of swap. An unknown, centralized host could keep everything received, never sending it out to other swappers. That's rare, but it has happened on some forums. In a decentralized swap, a few people might not complete their obligations. You could send out ten packets of fabric and receive nine back. When a quilter fails to follow through on a centralized swap, you receive a piece of the fabric or block that you sent, intended for that swapper, back from the hostess.

Postage is sometimes less for centralized swaps since all items are mailed to the same address. You do have to include a self-addressed stamped envelope for items to be returned to you. In a decentralized swap you pay for postage one way, but to multiple recipients.

Decentralized swaps are somewhat more personal because you can send a specific item to a specific swapper. That becomes more of an issue when you're swapping unique items, such as blocks that are made from a variety of fabrics. You cannot depend

ELSEWHERE ON THE WEB

▶ Another favorite decorative thread company is Sulky. They make all sorts of decorative and cotton threads, and the company's Web site offers lots of free projects that teach you exactly how to use them. Each type of thread is explained in detail, making the site an excellent resource for the quilting community. Visit www.sulky .com.

ASK YOUR GUIDE

What if I don't like the fabrics I receive in a swap?

▶ That can happen, but swap guidelines are very specific. You'll know what colors or types of fabrics are involved before you join. Keep an open mind when fabrics come back to you. We sometimes tend to buy the same types of fabrics over and over again instead of buying fabrics we need to build a usable assortment. Getting pieces from other quilters can help fill in the gaps.

on a centralized host to sort your blocks a certain way—it would be too time-consuming to do that for every swapper.

Centralized swaps have a bit of quality control built in. A hostess usually inspects swapped items before swapping them out with the group. Fabrics that are not cut correctly or blocks that are very poorly sewn are usually sent back to the person who mailed them. Our About.com quilting hosts are volunteers who manage swaps for fun, but they all feel they have a responsibility to monitor the quality of items that they mail out to their swappers.

There are a few risks when you swap, but overall I think you'll find that it's a fun and rewarding activity. You'll enjoy the discussions that are generated as each quilter receives her or his packets in the mail, and you'll make lots of new friends. Give it a try and I think you'll be hooked.

Always read and follow the swapping guidelines. Every quilt swap is accompanied by specific guidelines written by the host. Read them carefully and don't join the swap if you aren't sure you can abide by the rules. Guidelines differ for each individual swap, but there are a few things nearly all of them include:

- **A deadline.** Each swap ends on a specific date. Don't join the swap if you know you cannot comply. Hostesses will try to work with you if an emergency occurs after you've joined.
- **Fabric specifications.** A hostess might specify that you use LQS fabrics. That term stands for local quilt shop and indicates that you are expected to use all-cotton fabrics produced for quilters, which are typically of a higher quality than some types of fabrics found in discount stores and general fabric shops. If you aren't sure what's acceptable, ask.

- **Accurately cut fabric.** The fabric you submit for a swap must be cut accurately. Practice your rotary cutting skills before you join a fabric swap.
- **Block quality standards.** You'll be expected to sew accurate blocks that measure a specific size when they go into the mail. Make sure you cut patches accurately and sew an exact ¼" seam (covered in Chapter 7). If you need help, ask for it. The hostess and other swap members will offer advice. Hostesses do not expect perfection, but they do expect you to send items that meet the standards listed in the guidelines.
- **Prewashing requirements.** Fabric swaps nearly always specify that you prewash and press fabrics. You might be asked not to use scented fabric softeners since some people have problems with fragrances. Blocks should be assembled from prewashed fabrics.

Quilt swaps are about making friends, learning from others, and being part of a community. You'll receive blocks from quilters of every skill level. Some of the patches in a block might not be absolutely accurate, but when those blocks are all sewn together they'll make a lovely remembrance quilt. If you are a perfectionist and expect perfection from others, it might be best to stick with fabric swaps. If you do join block swaps, think "unique" instead of "imperfect" and you'll do just fine.

Show us your quilts. We have an online quilt show at the About.com Quilting site. The show is a series of galleries that are filled with quilts made by our forum members. Galleries are split up by theme. You'll find photos of quilts for kids, a gallery of star quilts,

quilts made to honor breast cancer survivors and raise money for research, art quilts, and many other kinds.

I hope you'll submit some of your quilts to the gallery, and I've started a new gallery just for quilts from this book. I know that our community would love to see how you interpret the patterns. See the Get Linked section for Web addresses.

Get Linked

Use these links to show us your quilts and to see quilts made by other members of the online quilting community.

SHOW YOUR QUILTS IN OUR GALLERIES

Use this form to submit your quilt to our online quilt show. Be sure to tell us a little bit about the quilt's background, such as what inspired you to make it.

http://about.com/quilting/submityours

QUILTS FROM THIS BOOK

I've created a special photo gallery just for quilts made from the patterns in this book. The gallery gives you a good look at the ways other quilters interpreted the patterns. Do share yours!

http://about.com/quilting/frombookgallery

The **ABOUT**.com *Guide to* **Quilting**

Chapter 2

Working with Fabrics and Colors

Choosing Colors for Your Quilts

We all have favorite colors. They show up in our homes, in our clothing, in our accessories—just about everywhere in our lives. When we make our first quilt, most of us choose fabrics in our favorite hues. They're our safety net: comfortable colors that make us feel at home.

Understanding color helps you select fabrics, even if you never break away from the comfort zone of your favorites. If you take the steps to understand color, you'll learn to mix colors to create movement and visual texture in your quilts. You'll have a better grasp of the different variations of each color, and that helps you discover ways to arrange colors for dramatic or subtle effects. I used to be confused and intimidated by the color wheel. I'm not real intuitive about choosing colors, so selecting and blending fabrics was always somewhat of a challenge when I tried to use the color wheel as a

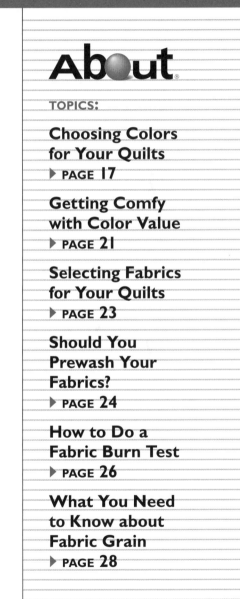

About.

guide. That's before I finally realized that sometimes it's best not to take color too seriously, and that a color wheel is simply a tool to help us understand the relationships between colors, not a device that dictates which colors we should use.

A **design wall** will be helpful as you work through this chapter. For a quick handmade design wall, tack up a piece of flannel or cotton batting onto the wall of your sewing room or where you have easy access to your quilting fabrics. Your fabrics will stay put on the material and you can step back and look at how the colors blend from afar.

Let's talk about color relationships and step through some of the different types of color arrangements. As we do you'll notice something: There's a theme for just about every color combination you could possibly devise. That means every color will work with any other color—a revelation that gives us a pretty good reason not to take color too seriously.

Start by looking at the primary colors. Blue, red, and yellow are known as primary colors. They are the building blocks for all other colors because you can mix them together in different ways to create every other color in the rainbow. You'll find primary colors arranged equal distances from each other on the most commonly used color wheel.

Secondary colors help explain how colors are mixed. Secondary colors are located midway between primary colors and are created by mixing together equal amounts of the primary colors that appear on either side of them.

- Green is made by combining blue and yellow.
- Orange is made by combining yellow and red.
- Violet is made by combining blue and red.

Tertiary colors fill out the color wheel. Tertiary colors complete the remaining six slots of a basic color wheel. Tertiary colors are created by combining equal parts of the primary and secondary colors that appear at their sides. Their names tell you which colors are used to create them.

- Yellow-green
- Yellow-orange
- Red-orange
- Red-violet
- Blue-violet
- Blue-green

There are different versions of pure colors. The colors you see on a basic color wheel are pure colors, made by combining equal amounts of the colors around them. Your fabrics will nearly always be hybrid variations of pure colors, and it's the variations that give us so many choices when it's time to make a quilt.

- **Shades** are colors created by adding different amounts of black to a color to make it darker.
- **Tones** are created by adding gray to colors. They are similar to the original colors, only more subdued.
- **Tints** are made by adding white to a color to make it lighter.

Have you ever noticed that some colors always stand out more than others? That's because some colors are more dominant than others—overpowering the colors around them. Color dominance is complex and depends on the specific combination of

TOOLS YOU NEED

▶ Buy a simple color wheel, available at nearly any art supply store. Check your local quilt shop for color wheels made especially for quilters, or view a color wheel online. You'll find a basic color wheel on my About.com Quilting Web site. Visit http://about.com/quilting/colorwheel.

fabrics in your quilt, but there are some guidelines you can use to predict how colors will interact.

- Yellow is the most dominant color.
- Pure colors are more dominant than tones that contain gray.
- Warm colors are more dominant than cool colors. Warm colors are on the right side of the wheel and include reds, yellows, and oranges.
- Dark fabrics are often more dominant than light fabrics unless they are competing with a warm color for attention.
- Very light fabrics used as accents often move forward in the design, becoming more dominant than darks.

Neutral colors give your eyes a place to rest. Neutral colors are weak versions of colors that give us a soft place to rest our eyes and allow other colors to control the design. We often use neutrals for backgrounds and for other areas of the quilt that we want to be less noticeable. All variations of white, gray, and beige are considered neutral. Black is a dark that can be dominant, but it's also a neutral when it provides a backdrop for vibrant colors.

Get acquainted with a few basic color arrangements. There are names for every type of color combination. Here are a few of the basics, always a good place to start when you make your first quilts. You can add neutrals to any of these color schemes.

- **Monochromatic color schemes**, also called one-color lay-outs, include all types of shades, tints, and tones of just one color. They can be challenging to make, but quite beautiful.

- **Analogous layouts** sound complicated, but the term simply refers to a color scheme made by using colors that are side by side on the color wheel. Analogous colors are a natural match because their color roots are similar.
- **Complementary themes** use colors that are located across from each other on the color wheel. They include combinations of red and green, yellow and purple, blue and orange, and variations of those colors. Sometimes it's best not to mix complementary colors in equal amounts. Use a sprinkling of one and larger amounts of the other.
- **Split complementary themes** include three colors that are side by side on the color wheel, plus the color that's directly across from the central color.

There are many more ways to structure colors, and truthfully, there are no bad color combinations. Look at all the gorgeous scrap quilts that have been made for generations. They often include all colors in the color wheel, in every tone, tint, and shade.

It's important to get comfortable with the color wheel, but let your imagination and creativity rule. Don't hesitate to experiment with color combinations. Try working with a color you don't think you like, because sometimes those little explorations out of our comfort zone help us find brand new favorites.

Getting Comfy with Color Value

I think color value is more important than color. Value refers to how light or dark a color is in comparison with another color, a critical characteristic when we want our fabrics to blend together or contrast with each other to define a design. Fabric patches emerge or recede in the design depending in part on the arrangement of value. One of the best ways to experiment with color value is to gather a stack of fabrics and experiment with them on your design wall.

ELSEWHERE ON THE WEB

▶ Color and color value allow us to create optical illusions in our quilts. Gloria Hansen (www.gloriahansen .com) is a master at combining fabrics to create visual depth and illusion—and she creates nearly all of the unique fabrics used in her quilts. Karen Combs (www.karencombs.com) has stitched lots of optical illusion quilts, and she has written books and patterns to help you learn her techniques.

1. Sort several colors of fabrics from dark to light and tack them up next to each other on a neutral wall. Step back. Do the fabrics blend together as they progress along the wall, or do some of them stand out and interrupt the flow? Rearrange the fabrics and check again.

    It is not unusual if fabrics still don't flow perfectly from light to dark. It's easy to sort fabrics when they are the same color, but it becomes more complicated when you add color warmth and other dominance factors.

2. Refer to the guidelines for color dominance that we talked about earlier in this chapter and sort again, moving warm colors into place as needed with the darks.

    Sometimes it's difficult to judge the color value of printed fabrics, especially florals and larger prints, because value changes depending on which part of the fabric appears in the quilt. Some cuts might be light, while other areas are dark. Always keep that characteristic in mind when you're selecting printed fabrics.

You're in total control of the dark and light starting points for your quilts. Place a medium green next to a white patch and it's a dark. Sew it next to black and it becomes a medium—or even a light. If a pattern calls for a dark fabric it's up to you to choose where you want your darks to begin. Lightening up on the darks simply means you'll choose lighter lights to sew beside them.

Learn how to preview color value. There are several easy ways to do this. You can use a computer drawing program to make an outline drawing of your quilt, then fill in areas with light to dark shades of gray.

View your fabrics with a value filter, usually made from transparent red, green, or pink pieces of plastic. The filters mask color and allow you to view the fabrics in shades of gray. Filters aren't a sure thing, because different filter colors alter warm and cool colors differently.

Try using a scanner or copier to make black-and-white copies of fabrics. It's a lot easier to sort fabrics when you take away color's influence. Another trick is to view your sorted fabrics from a distance. Squint your eyes or look at them through a peephole—like the little magnifying glasses we put in a door so that we can see who's outside before we open it. Turn the peephole around and look at it backwards for a distant view of the fabrics.

Pay attention to quilts you see at quilt shows and on the Internet. Analyze them. What do you like or dislike most? Would any of the arrangements work for the quilt you're making?

The real key to color-value success is practice and experimentation. Arrange fabrics to contrast with each other. Sort them again and force them to blend. Keep working on it and it won't be long until you know instinctively which fabrics to combine to get the effects you're looking for.

Selecting Fabrics for Your Quilts

There will be times when you decide to work with different types of fabrics, but it's usually best to start out by sewing with traditional quilting cottons. They are durable and easier to handle than somewhat slippery polyester blends. If you decide to join quilt fabric and block swaps, cotton fabrics will nearly always be a requirement.

Before you shop for fabric or read a pattern, get familiar with popular fabrics and some of the basic terms used to describe them:

- Floral prints are probably the most plentiful fabric in quilt shops. You'll find floral fabrics in every color and every scale, from tiny prints to flowers with bold splashes of color.

TOOLS YOU NEED

▶ Martingale and Company manufactures a tool called the Ruby Beholder. It's a rectangle made from dark red transparent plastic. Hold the filter up to your eyes and look at your fabrics. The red color masks other colors and helps you view fabrics in shades of black and gray. Enter ruby beholder in the Search window at www .martingale-pub.com. Some of the quilters on our forums use a transparent red report cover to help them sort fabrics by value. You can buy report covers at office supply stores.

▶ Nearly all traditional Amish quilts are made with solid fabrics, not prints. Colors vary depending on the region the quilts came from, since some Amish groups allowed colors that other groups did not use. Amish quilters often mix small amounts of very light fabrics into their quilts, creating an effect called sparkle. The Revere Collection's Web site includes a stunning gallery of Amish quilts. Visit www .revere-collection.com/dir_ nii/nii_esprit.html.

- Geometric prints have motifs that are based on designs like circles, squares, triangles, and diamonds.
- Stripes and plaid designs can be printed on the fabric, or they can be created by weaving the fabric with different colored threads. Woven stripes and plaids are called home-spuns and yarn-dyed fabrics.
- Tone-on-tone fabrics look like solids from a distance, but when you get closer you see that they are printed fabrics designed with different variations of the same color.
- Conversational prints, sometimes called novelty prints, depict real objects, such as insects or animals, children, clothing, cars, teacups—the list is endless.
- Hand-dyed fabrics and their variations are unique fabrics with mottled colors and designs.

Successful quilts are usually made with a combination of fabric types, so mix away. You'll be surprised how well different fabrics combine to make a stunning quilt.

Should You Prewash Your Fabrics?

Some quilters never prewash their fabrics, but I nearly always do because it prevents nasty little surprises that can occur when I wash a quilt the first time. Some cotton fabrics bleed, losing their dyes in the wash. Reds, purples, and other vivid colors are usually the worst culprits. It's best to find out if they bleed now before they transfer dyes onto the patches of your finished quilt. Crocking is a similar problem, but it occurs when dry fabrics touch each other and loose particles of dye transfer onto neighboring fabrics.

Sewing unwashed fabrics together could create other problems the first time you wash the finished quilt. What if the fabrics in the quilt shrink differently? Uneven shrinkage can cause lots of uneven puckers across the entire quilt.

Unwashed quilting fabrics are coated with sizing, protective coatings, and other chemicals. They make the fabrics feel crisp, protect them the fading rays of the sun and lights, and make the fabrics easy to rotary cut. However, handling coated fabrics or breathing small particles of chemical dust that flakes off of them could be a health risk for sensitive individuals.

Prewashing the fabric removes most of the chemicals. You can make the fabric stiffer again by spraying on sizing or starch. It's another chemical, but it's one you can control. Read the ingredients list on the can to find out exactly what's in it.

Here is one method to prewash your fabrics. I like to wash my quilting fabrics in cool water with either a mild detergent or Orvus paste, a soap that's made especially for quilts. It isn't necessary to agitate the fabrics. Let them soak for a bit then move the dial to spin to remove the water. Repeat to rinse. Eliminating agitation helps cut down on frayed and tangled fabric edges that can become a problem during a wash.

Pop the damp fabrics into the dryer and dry on a low setting. Remove them when dry and fold neatly. There's no need to press until you're ready to use each fabric.

Do a simple bleed test to find unstable fabric dyes. Fabrics made by companies that cater to quilters are pretty stable and do not usually bleed, but until you know which fabrics you can trust, it's a good idea to bleed test the vivid fabrics in your collection before you use them. Pay special attention to deep purples, violets, and reds.

Here is how to do a bleed test:

▶ Use Synthropol, a liquid additive that helps keep loose dyes from accumulating on other fabrics in the wash, when you prewash your fabrics. Synthropol won't keep one patch in a quilt from absorbing dye from its neighbor, but it will help protect unsewn fabrics when you wash a batch to check for bleeding. Synthropol is available from most suppliers who sell fabric dyes, including Dharma Trading at http://dharmatrading.com.

1. Fill a clear, 2-cup glass measuring cup with warm water and put in a little bit of the same soap you use to wash your quilting fabrics.
2. Clip off a small swatch of the fabric you'd like to test and place it in the soap solution. Allow it to sit in the liquid for fifteen minutes or so.
3. Check to see if the water is discolored. If the water is tinted, it means the fabric bleeds and could possibly stain other fabrics in the wash.
4. Do one more test. Remove the patch from the water and place it on a white paper towel. Inspect the swatch in about thirty minutes. Is the towel discolored? That's what will happen to adjacent patches in a quilt before the quilt has a chance to dry.
5. Rinse out the soap and dry the fabric swatch. Perform the bleed test again. If it still bleeds, do not use the fabric in a project that will be washed.

How to Do a Fabric Burn Test

Earlier in this chapter we talked a little bit about using only cotton fabrics in your quilts, but do you know how to determine if a fabric is cotton? You might find a nice fabric on eBay or at a flea market. Or maybe you've received a questionable fabric from a nonquilting friend or in a swap. A burn test will help you determine what types of fibers are in unknown fabrics. Be sure to perform the test outside on a calm day, or in a well-ventilated and fireproof area inside.

Cut small swatches of the fabrics you want to test—1½" squares should work just fine. Find a flameproof container, such as an ashtray. Gather a few matches or another source of a flame. You'll also need tweezers or a hemostat to grasp some fabrics while they burn.

Here is how to conduct a burn test:

1. Place a fabric swatch in your fireproof container and use a small flame to ignite one corner of it.
2. Pay attention to the smoke as the fabric burns. Burning cotton smells like burning paper, but an odor similar to burning feathers means the fabric might be wool or silk. Wool burns more easily than silk.
3. A dark plume of smoke that smells like burning plastic probably indicates that the fabric contains polyester.
4. Let the ashes cool and examine them. Cotton ashes are soft and turn to dust when touched. Burned wool looks like black, brittle beads and crushes between your fingers. Irregular, hard lumps are the remains of melted synthetics.
5. Do one more test. Unravel a clump of threads from a bit more of the fabric. Hold it away from you with tweezers and slowly move a flame toward the threads. Cotton will ignite as the flame draws near. Synthetic threads curl away from the heat and begin to melt. Rayon continues to burn after the flame is removed; it has an odor similar to cotton but does not produce an afterglow as cotton does. Linen fibers burn like cotton and smell like cotton, but linen burns more slowly.

Do burn tests of fabrics you know are made from cotton or other specific fibers. Watch the results carefully so that you'll know what to expect when you test unknown fibers.

ASK YOUR GUIDE

Do you use fabric softener on your quilting cottons?

▶ I usually put a very small amount of an unscented liquid fabric softener in the rinse water when I wash quilting fabrics. I join fabric and block swaps online and some quilters are overly sensitive to scent. One-fourth to one-third of a capful of unscented softener keeps static cling at bay but isn't enough to create problems for those quilters.

▶ If your water contains
chlorine that's strong enough
to produce an odor there's a
chance it could fade your fabrics, especially after repeated
washings. Neutralize the
chlorine by putting about ½
cup of vinegar in your washing machine's wash and rinse
water. The smell of vinegar
won't be noticeable in the
dry fabrics.

What You Need to Know about Fabric Grain

The term grain refers to the arrangement of threads in a piece of cloth. It's a simple arrangement, with some threads that run across the fabric and some along its length. Understanding **fabric grain**—and putting it to work for you—is one of the best ways I know to sew accurate quilt blocks.

Let's look at grain components. Long threads are stretched on a loom and secured. They're called warp threads and they become the fabric's **lengthwise grain**—the grain that runs along the fabric as it comes off of the bolt.

Shorter threads, called weft threads, are woven back and forth across the long threads. These threads make up the fabric's **crosswise grain** and form bound edges called **selvages** as they turn back and forth during the weave. Fabrics are more tightly woven for about a half inch from the selvages inward to keep the edges from fraying while the fabric is on the bolt.

Both the lengthwise and crosswise grain are regarded as straight grain—sometimes called straight-of-grain. Patches cut with their edges along either straight grain are less likely to stretch out of shape as you handle them because the network of threads offers the edges a bit of support. The lengthwise-grain threads are less stretchy than crosswise-grain threads.

Another term you'll hear when you cut quilting patches is **bias**, which refers to any cut edge that does not run along a straight grain.

True bias is defined as the direction at a 45-degree angle to the straight grains, but in quilting we refer to any cut that doesn't run along a straight grain as a bias cut. There are no threads to stabilize a bias edge, so it's quite stretchy.

Be sure to handle all fabric patches carefully, even straight-grain pieces. They're far less likely to stretch out of shape than bias-edge pieces, but they are not indestructible.

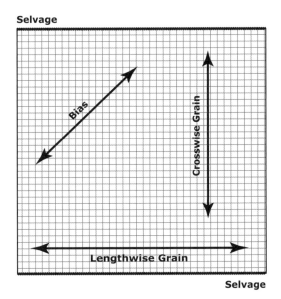

Fig. 2-1 A look at fabric grain

Here's why fabric grain is important. Consider this quilt-making scenario: You must cut setting and corner triangles to fill in the gaps around the outer edges of the Shades of the Past quilt in Chapter 15. Both types of triangles look just alike, but the long edges of the larger **setting triangles** end up on the outer perimeter of the quilt. The short edges of the corner triangles are on the quilt's outer edges.

The outer edges of a quilt are prone to stretch, so they're the last place you want to sew long triangle edges cut on the stretchy bias. The same is true for the corners—you don't want stretchy edges at each corner of the quilt.

There's a simple solution. Cut setting triangles by slicing a large square in half twice diagonally. Assuming the sides of the square are cut along the straight grains, the diagonal cuts produce four triangles with the grain on their long edges. Corner triangles are created by cutting a square in half once diagonally to produce triangles with the straight grain on their short edges. You'll learn how to determine sizes for these triangles in Chapter 4.

Fig. 2-2 Cutting setting and corner triangles

Learn how to determine which straight grain is "best."
Fabric edges cut along the lengthwise grain are quite a bit less stretchy than crosswise-grain strips. There are a few reasons why:

- Warp threads were firmly attached to the loom while weft threads were woven through them. The loom held the threads firmly in place and enhanced their structure, and the interlacing of weft threads gives them strength.
- Most fabrics have more warp threads per square inch than weft threads, making the warp stronger.

Because they have minimal stretch, lengthwise-grain strips make wonderful quilt borders and sashing. In Chapter 4 you'll learn how to use lengthwise-grain border strips to square up the edges of a skewed block or quilt top.

Crosswise-grain strips are the cuts most often used for strip piecing, a technique that helps you assemble quilts quickly and accurately. If crosswise-grain strips stretch too much, switch to lengthwise-grain cuts and your accuracy will improve. Read directions for strip piecing in Chapter 7.

Stretchy bias edges are a problem when they end up along a block's outer edge, but the same stretch is perfect when **binding** must be sewn around a quilt's curved, outer edge. Bias cuts come in handy for other quilting components, including long stems made for appliqué quilts.

Triangles always have at least one bias edge. Analyze your quilt to decide where that edge should be placed. You'll find that most bias edges are sewn to straight-grain edges within the interior of the quilt.

Perform a stretch test to get a feel for fabric grain. There's no better way to become accustomed to fabric grain than to do this simple stretch test. It will help you visualize just how much stretch you'll find along different portions of the fabric. Another plus—you'll be able to identify the lengthwise and crosswise grain in scrap patches with no selvages.

Here is how to perform a stretch test:

1. Cut a 3" square of cotton fabric with its edges parallel to the straight grains.
2. Tug on the patch from side to side in either direction. Now switch sides and tug from the opposite direction. Did you feel a difference? The square probably had less give from one direction. That was the lengthwise grain.
3. Tug on the square from corner to corner—go ahead and give it a good tug! I'll bet it stretched quite a bit, and it might even be permanently distorted. That was the bias. It doesn't take a whole lot of handling to stretch a bias edge out of shape.

Experiment with fabric grain as you make your quilts. Before long you'll have a much better understanding of the best ways to place grain in your quilts in order to achieve the results you're looking for.

ASK YOUR GUIDE

I only have a little bit of fabric left—not enough to cut patch edges on the straight grain. What should I do?

▶ There will be times when you must sew a bias edge in a position that doesn't enhance the structure of the quilt. This time it's because you only have a little bit of fabric, but the next time you might want to place the print a certain way within the triangle. Don't worry about it—go ahead and sew the patches together. Handle the edge carefully until you give it a bit of extra strength by sewing it to another component.

Get Linked

Visit my About.com Quilting site to find more information and illustrations that will help you work with color.

TOP BOOKS ABOUT COLOR

Here's a selection of excellent books about color. These books are all written especially for quilters.

http://about.com/quilting/booksoncolor

COLOR WHEEL BASICS FOR QUILTERS

This step-by-step description of working with a color wheel is accompanied by illustrations of various color layouts.

http://about.com/quilting/colorwheelbasics

Chapter 3

Inspired by Design

Developing Your Own Style

If you give ten quilters the same quilt pattern, you'll be amazed when you see their finished quilts. They'll all be different unless for some reason the quilters collaborated to make identical projects. That's because when we work with patterns we nearly always find a way to include our own favorite fabrics and colors. We may follow the pattern closely, but there are always opportunities to break away and add a bit of our own personal style.

Give ten more quilters thirty identical quilt blocks to use in a quilt and you'll see even more variation in their finished projects, because they'll all choose a different way to sew them together. Some will place the blocks side by side along their straight edges, either alone or with pieced or plain strips between them. Some quilters will arrange the blocks **on point**—with their corners pointing up and down. They'll all choose different borders. Some will use one border and others will sew on multiples. And even something as simple as variety in the outer binding can make a huge difference in the final look of the quilt.

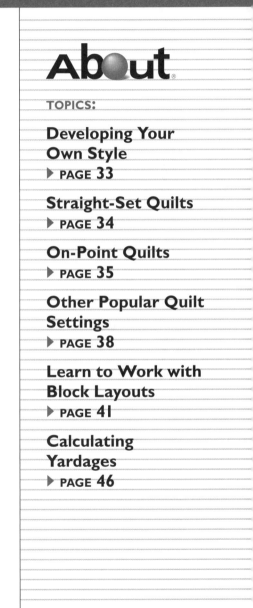

About.

▶ Design tools vary depending on the ways each quilter works. As mentioned earlier, a design wall, made by hanging flannel on an open wall, will help you position blocks and fabric pieces with ease. A ruler, graph paper, and lead pencil are helpful for quilters who like to jot down ideas by hand. A generic computer drawing program might be more your style—or a software program developed especially for quilters. Keep a calculator handy for figuring block and component sizes.

It's those personal choices that have helped keep quilting a popular art form for so long. It wouldn't be near as much fun to stitch the same things over and over again with no regard to your own creativity. Beginning quilters are just as likely as anyone else to create a smashing style on their very first try.

The choices you'll make when you design a quilt all fall under the broad area of settings, sometimes referred to simply as sets. The term means design or layout. When you break away from a printed pattern in some way you'll find that it's easy to create a unique quilt. Use the ideas and instructions in this chapter to make changes to any quilt pattern. It won't be long before you are comfortable designing a quilt from scratch—all by yourself.

Straight-Set Quilts

Straight-set quilts have blocks that are arranged in vertical and horizontal rows. The straight edges of square or rectangular blocks are arranged with their flat sides pointing up, down, and to each side. Blocks are placed in horizontal rows and then the blocks in each row are sewn together. The rows are then attached to each other to complete the quilt top.

The blocks in your straight-set quilt do not have to be identical. They can be the same blocks but sewn from a variety of fabrics, a layout we refer to as scrappy. The blocks can all be different, making it a sampler quilt. You might choose two blocks that look good together and alternate them from row to row. One block in that scenario would be called an alternate block. You might also choose to sew a plain fabric square between the blocks—a quick and easy way to increase quilt size without making more blocks.

Straight-set blocks often have plain or pieced sashing between them. Sashing acts as a block divider and adds a new design element as it increases the size of the quilt. You'll read more about sashing in Chapter 4.

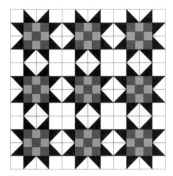

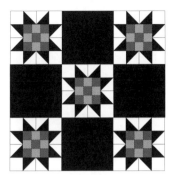

Fig. 3-1 Straight-set quilt with blocks sewn side by side

Fig. 3-2 Straight-set quilt alternated with plain squares

On-Point Quilts

An on-point setting is created by positioning quilt blocks so that their corners point up and down and to the sides. On-point blocks are arranged by sewing blocks in diagonal rows. Plain or pieced triangles, called setting triangles, fill in the gaps along angled edges and corners where rows end. The Shades of the Past quilt in Chapter 15 is an example of an on-point set.

Fig. 3-3 Shades of the Past is an on-point quilt

Plain setting squares are an excellent place to display your quilting skills. Fill them with any type of quilting motif you like, including winding vines adorned with flowers and leaves, gentle scallops placed equal distances apart, or straight lines that intersect each other at an angle.

Like straight-set quilts, you can add plain squares between blocks or use a mixture of quilt blocks in an on-point setting. The setting triangles can be cut from plain fabric, pieced partial blocks, or even adorned with appliqué.

Learn to cut setting and corner triangles for on-point quilts. Take a look back at the layout for the Shades of the Past quilt. The triangles around its sides are larger than the corner triangles, but they're all the same shape—half of a square. It's one of those cases where looks are deceiving, because the side and corner triangles are cut using different methods.

We talked about fabric grain in Chapter 2. On-point layouts give us an opportunity to put grain characteristics to work to create patches that will help stabilize the quilt. Remember the guideline about stretchy bias edges—we rarely place them around the outer edges of any component. Instead, we sew them to a straight-grain edge whenever possible.

That's one reason we nearly always cut squares with the straight grains running parallel to their straight edges. Straight grains don't stretch very much, so our squares tend to stay fairly intact as we work with them, and their edges make perfect stabilizers for the stretchy triangles that are often sewn to them.

What if we created our side setting triangles by cutting a square in half once diagonally, from one corner to the opposite corner? That cut produces a triangle with straight-grain edges on its short sides—the old sides of the square—and a stretchy bias cut along its new long edge.

Look at the layout for the Shades of the Past quilt again. To prevent stretch, the long edges of the setting triangles should be straight-grain cuts, not bias edges, so cutting a square in half once won't work. There's an easy solution—cut the setting triangles by slicing oversized squares twice diagonally to produce triangles with the straight grain on their longest edges.

The short edges of the corner triangle rest along the outside of the quilt—a good place for straight-grain edges. Cutting a square in half is the perfect way to make corner triangles. The long stretchy edges are sewn to the side of a quilt block, where they become stabilized by straight-grain patches.

Fig. 3-4 Corner triangles, left; setting triangles, right

There are a few simple formulas you can use to cut corner and setting triangles:

Cutting Corner Triangles

Find the finished diagonal by multiplying your block's **finished size** x 1.41

Parent square size = finished diagonal/2 + 0.875"; round up to nearest ⅛"

Example: Finished block size = 12"

12" x 1.41 = 16.92" (finished diagonal)

Parent square size = 16.92"/2 = 8.46" + 0.875" = 9.34"; round up to 9⅜"

So, cut a 9⅜" square, and then cut it in half once diagonally to make corner triangles for 12" square blocks.

▶ Computerized quilting programs include predrawn quilt blocks that can be arranged in any way you like. Tell the program what type of layout you like and it creates it instantly. Some programs even include scanned images of real fabrics that you can use to fill in the patches of the quilt. Two popular programs are Electric Quilt, which is Windows compatible (www.electric quilt.com), and Quilt-Pro, which can be used on either a Mac or Windows system (www.quiltpro.com).

Cutting Setting Triangles

Parent square size = finished diagonal + 1.25"; round up to nearest ⅛"

Example for setting triangles adjacent to 12" squares

Parent square size = 16.92" (from finished diagonal in equation above) + 1.25" = 18.17", rounded up to 18.25" or 18¼"

Cut an 18¼" square, and then cut it twice diagonally to produce four setting triangles with the straight grain on their longest edges.

SETTING COMPONENTS FOR POPULAR BLOCK SIZES

Finished Block Size	Setting Squares	Squares for Setting Triangles	Squares for Corner Triangles
4" x 4"	4½" x 4½"	7" x 7"	3¾" x 3¾"
6" x 6"	6½" x 6½"	9¾" x 9¾"	5⅛" x 5⅛"
9" x 9"	9½" x 9½"	14" x 14"	7¼" x 7¼"
10" x 10"	10½" x 10½"	15⅜" x 15⅜"	8" x 8"
12" x 12"	12½" x 12½"	18¼" x 18¼"	9⅜" x 9⅜"
14" x 14"	14½" x 14½"	21" x 21"	10¾" x 10¾"
15" x 15"	15½" x 15½"	22½" x 22½"	11½" x 11½"
18" x 18"	18½" x 18½"	26¾" x 26¾"	13¾" x 13¾"

Other Popular Quilt Settings

Medallion settings have a focal center that's surrounded by a series of triangles or borders that relate to and enhance the quilt's design. The center medallion can be made from one large pieced or appliquéd block, or it can be a cluster of blocks that are sewn together.

Medallion centers are often placed on point, then framed by triangles. Quilters sometimes like to place a row of blocks against the outer edges of the framing triangles. If the sides of your medallion are an odd size that's not easy to match with quilt blocks, you can even it up by adding one or two borders. For instance, if the center medallion unit measures 14" on each edge, its finished size is 13½" after subtracting the seam allowances. Make it finish at 15" square by adding 1¼" wide border strips (¾" finished width plus ½" for seams) to each side. You can then sew an even number of 5" finished blocks to the sides of the medallion.

Fig. 3-5 Medallion quilt example

Strippy quilts have blocks that are sewn into vertical columns. Strippy quilts have been popular for a very long time and are made up of quilt blocks sewn in vertical rows. If quilt blocks are straight set, then long, continuous strips of fabric are sewn to the sides of the rows to separate them before rows are joined. Strips are not sewn horizontally between blocks.

If strippy blocks are set on point, setting triangles are used to fill in the gaps at their corners and sides before the rows are joined to form a column.

ELSEWHERE ON THE WEB

▶ Grandmother's Flower Garden quilts were extremely popular during the 1930s and 1940s. As happens today, many quilters from those eras didn't finish their projects. These projects are known as a UFO, for "unfinished object." Search www.eBay.com for the term grandmother's flower garden and you'll nearly always find vintage blocks and unquilted tops that can be purchased at reasonable prices. Finishing a vintage quilt is a wonderful way to learn a new skill and preserve a piece of the past.

Tessellating quilt layouts are designs that use a single, interlocking shape throughout the entire quilt. No filler patches are used to make the designs match up with each other. Patches are usually turned horizontally or vertically to snap them into place—kind of like a large jigsaw puzzle made from a single shape. You can learn more about tessellation at http://about.com/quilting/ tessellation.

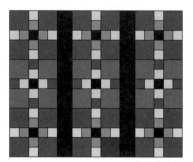

Fig. 3-6 Example of strippy quilt

Zigzag-set quilts are similar to strippy quilts. Zigzag-set blocks are placed on point and in columns, but the setting triangles that surrounded each column are offset from each other and sewn with different colors or color values to make the layout look jagged. These quilts are sometimes called streak o' lightning quilts.

Fig. 3-7 A zigzag quilt

One-patch quilts are made by repeating a single shape. Three popular one-patch quilt designs are Grandmother's Flower Garden, Tumbling Blocks, and Thousand Pyramids. These quilts are each sewn using just one shape, and color as well as color value are critical for their success. Half and quarter portions of the shapes are used to fill in gaps around the outer edges of one-patch quilts.

Fig. 3-8 One-patch quilt example

Learn to Work with Block Layouts

When we design a quilt that has more than one type of block in it we usually want the edges of both block designs to look good where they meet when the quilt is sewn together. It's easy to make your blocks flow nicely into one another once you understand the basic structure and terms used to describe patchwork blocks.

Quilt blocks all have names, like Log Cabin, Snowball, Shooting Star, Monkey Wrench—the list is endless. But quilt blocks are also referred to by the categories that describe their structure. You might have heard the terms four patch, five patch, seven patch, and nine patch. There are thousands of blocks that fall into each of those categories and they all have something in common—the basic grid that forms the backbone of each block type is the same.

As you work with quilt blocks, keep in mind that their initial grids are a starting point. They can be subdivided into more grids, but their basic framework stays the same. After a bit of practice you'll recognize any type of patchwork block, and that's a skill that will help you design quilts with ease.

ELSEWHERE ON THE WEB

▶ The Henry Ford Museum in Dearborn, Michigan, has an extensive collection of quilts. A group of quilts sewn between 1770 and 1990 are displayed in the museum's online quilt show (www.the henryford.org/museum/ quiltinggenius). If you like the quilts you might want to explore the book *Fons and Porter Presents Quilts from the Henry Ford*, by Marianne Fons and Liz Porter, which features a collection of twenty-four quilts on display in the museum.

Four-patch blocks are among the most commonly used quilt blocks. The backbone of a four-patch block is made up of four equal squares, two across and two down. You can make four-patch blocks just like that, or subdivide them in thousands of ways.

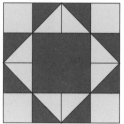

Fig. 3-9 Examples of four-patch blocks

Nine-patch blocks are the other most commonly used quilt block. Before we subdivide them, they contain nine equal squares, three across and three down. It's easy to subdivide a nine-patch block, and the majority of quilts made with them will contain versions that are more intricate than the basic nine-square structure.

Fig. 3-10 Examples of nine-patch blocks

Five-patch blocks are more intricate from the beginning. Five-patch blocks have a gridwork of twenty-five equal squares, five across and five down. Their grids are already

▶ I like to keep an eye out for printed cloth bags that hold tea, grains, and other food items. Most of these bags are colorfast and can be worked into a quilt. Some are very colorful. You'll find printed bags in gift shops and food specialty shops, especially around the winter holidays.

somewhat intricate, so they aren't subdivided as often as other quilt blocks.

Fig. 3-11 Examples of five-patch blocks

Seven-patch blocks have even more grids. Seven-patch blocks have a grid made up of forty-nine equal squares, seven across and seven down. Like five-patch blocks, they are not usually divided into additional grids.

Fig. 3-12 Examples of seven-patch blocks

Use your knowledge of grids to design a quilt. When you sew different types of blocks side-by-side you usually want their small patchwork units to match up along seams. Blocks that link in that way give the quilt the illusion of movement, because fabrics seem to flow together along the matched lines. That effect is easier to achieve if both blocks in the quilt have the same basic patch structure.

ELSEWHERE ON THE WEB

▶ One of our forum hostesses hosts a patchwork swap every month called Beginner Block Lotto. Enter as many blocks as you like and you'll have a chance to win the blocks made by other quilters. There's a new block each month and they usually follow a theme. Even if you don't want to participate, I think you'll be inspired by previous blocks sewn by the online quilting community. Visit http://blocksnswaps.blogspot.com.

Let's look at a few examples. If you sew a four-patch block next to a five-patch block the units won't match evenly along their sides, even if you experiment with size. That look might be just fine with you, but it's an important trait to consider when you're working on your design. You might find a more pleasing match by selecting a second four-patch block that blends with and looks perfect with the first.

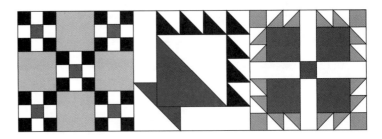

Fig. 3-13 Examples of matched and mismatched blocks

Now that you understand block grids, it's easy to choose a size for your quilt blocks. The majority of us cut our quilting patches with a rotary cutter. There are times you'll use templates—rigid pattern pieces that you'll learn about in Chapter 8—but most of the block sizes you choose will be determined by how easy it is to rotary cut them.

Sometimes it's easier to choose a size for our individual grids, then multiply it by the grids across and down to choose a size. Let's say you want to make a nine-patch block with individual grids that are 3" square. You know there are three units across and three down. Three times three equals nine—the finished size of your block. So what would the finished size of a five-patch block be if its units are 3" square? That's easy, three times five equals fifteen.

You can approach block sizes from the opposite direction if you like. You want to make a 10" square five-patch block. That would work, because its units would finish at 2" square—ten divided by five equals two. What about a 10" seven-patch block? Ten divided by seven equals 1.42. That's not a size that can be rotary cut with accuracy. Choose a unit size that you can cut with ease—1½". Multiplying it by ten, your block would finish at 11½" square.

Play with the numbers until you find the ideal size for your quilt. Remember that the smallest division on rotary cutting rulers is ⅛", so steer clear of dimensions that are in smaller increments. Any finished size that you can rotary cut with ease will remain easy to cut after you add a seam allowance. We'll talk about seam allowances in Chapter 7.

Use this decimal conversion chart to easily switch back and forth from your calculator to the numbers on your rotary ruler.

DECIMAL CONVERSIONS

Decimal Figure	Ruler Measurement
.125	⅛
.25	¼
.375	⅜
.5	½
.625	⅝
.75	¾

There's an easy way to make blocks with different numbers of grids finish at the same size. To mix blocks with different grid structures you'll need to find a finished size that works with both layouts. Nine-patch blocks and four-patch blocks can both finish at 12" square because it's easy to rotary cut their grids when divided into that number. Twelve divided by four equals three—the side dimensions of your four-patch units. Twelve divided by three equals four—the side dimensions of your nine-patch units.

ASK YOUR GUIDE

I'm making a quilt with different blocks that were sent to me by several people. How can I arrange them if their grids don't match?

▶ That happens often with friendship blocks, and sometimes you even plan it yourself when you make a sampler quilt, which has different blocks in every position. If you don't like the way blocks look when you place them next to each other, sew plain pieces of narrow sashing between them to minimize the differences. Another option is to sew a setting square between the blocks. Put the blocks on a design wall and experiment a bit to see if a layout speaks to you. Read about sashing in Chapter 4.

A five-patch block and a nine-patch block can both finish at 15", because their side grids, five and three, divide evenly into fifteen.

Unit and block dimensions do not have to be in whole numbers. Combine numbers to create blocks that can be easily cut with your rotary cutter.

Calculating Yardages

Calculating exactly how much fabric you need for a specific quilt design is easy if you plan to use a limited number of fabrics in the quilt, but it's a little trickier when you make a scrap quilt out of many fabrics. When you figure yardages, always purchase more than the calculated amounts to compensate for shrinkage and to cover any mistakes that must be corrected. I almost always add a quarter yard to all of my calculations—often more if the cuts I must make from the fabric are large.

Start by designing your quilt on graph paper or with one of the computerized quilting software programs such as Electric Quilt or Quilt-Pro. If you use a software program it will calculate yardages for you. If you draw it on graph paper or with generic drawing software you'll need to calculate it yourself.

Color-code components in the quilt so that you'll know exactly which fabrics will be used in different areas. Determine the unfinished dimensions of each different object. Jot down all the different color codes and begin building your yardage requirement.

How many of the first identical object do you need? Let's use sashing as an example. Say your quilt contains eighteen sashing strips that are each 2" × 6" long. The strips are sewn vertically between blocks. Five rows of 2" × 28½" sashing are sewn horizontally between rows.

You can cut seven 2" × 6" strips from each 2" strip that's cut across the fabric's crosswise grain. You can cut one 2" × 28½" strip across the straight grain, and if your fabric is wide enough you can

ELSEWHERE ON THE WEB

▶ Charm quilts are made up of hundreds or even thousands of different fabrics, one piece of each, and typically sewn into a one-patch quilt using a square, a rectangle, a triangle, or another single shape. It's easy to accumulate fabrics for a charm quilt when you organize a fabric swap with your online or offline friends. Sophie Junction offers a peek at outgoing and incoming fabrics in a recent swap. You might be surprised by the variety at her Web site, http://blocks nswaps.blogspot.com/2006/09/before-after.html.

cut two short sashing strips from the excess length of long strips. Here's how it works out:

- ○ Cut two 2" × 42" crosswise grain strips, then cut seven 2" x 6" strips from each for fourteen short sashing
- ○ Cut five 2" × 42" crosswise grain strips, then cut five 2" x 28½" strips from each for long sashing
- ○ Cut the four remaining 2" x 6" sashing strips from the tails leftover from cutting long strips

You've cut a total of five 2" strips from your fabric, or 10". Divide the total number of inches required, 10, by the length of a yard in inches, 36. The result is .28 yard, or slightly over ¼ yard. I would probably purchase ½ yard of fabric.

To cut lengthwise grain strips, you would need at least 28½" of fabric on the lengthwise grain, or 28½ divided by 36, or ⅞ yard of fabric. You would have quite a bit of leftover fabric to use in other projects.

Use this same technique to calculate all required yardages. Remember to:

- Figure unfinished sizes, which include seam allowances.
- Calculate how many identical components you need.
- Divide one side of the component's dimension into the width of your fabric to determine how many cuts will be required.
- Multiply the number of cuts by the dimension you'll cut to determine how many inches of continuous fabric are required.
- Divide the inches required by thirty-six, the length of a yard, to determine yardage requirement.
- Buy a little more than the amount calculated.

▶ Mock up a quilt block by scanning a portion of each fabric you plan to use into the computer at 100 percent. Print the scanned fabrics on paper and then cut out the patches for the block, eliminating seam allowances. Use a glue stick to attach the patches to a large sheet of blank newsprint or other paper. Step back and take a look. Do you like what you see? If you do, that's great. If you don't, you haven't wasted any fabric and can experiment a bit more before you sew.

Be sure to make the same calculations for each use of a fabric. Combine cuts when you can to conserve fabric. There's no need to make cuts across the entire crosswise grain if you only need a few pieces of a certain size. Simply cut those from the leading edge of fabric and use the remainder for other components.

Here's a handy table that converts inches to yards. Most quilting fabrics are at least 42" wide after prewashing and removing selvages. Some flannels and other fabrics are narrower. Most denim fabrics are 60" wide.

COMMON FABRIC INCHES TO YARDS CONVERSIONS

Yardage Designation	Inches of Fabric
⅛ yard	4½"
¼ yard	9"
⅓ yard	11⅞"
½ yard	18"
⅝ yard	22½"
⅔ yard	23¾"
¾ yard	27"
⅞ yard	31½"

Use this easy method to estimate fabric requirements. It isn't as exact, but you can estimate fabric requirements another way. Calculate the size of your quilt minus its borders, and figure the yardage required to make the backing with traditional quilting cottons—not special backing fabrics. Increase the yardage by one-half—if you need ten yards, increase it to fifteen. See Chapter 9 for backing calculation instructions.

Determine how many fabrics you'll use in the quilt and in what proportions. For instance, perhaps you plan to use five fabrics. Two will be used in 20 percent of the quilt each, one will be used in 33 percent of the quilt, and two more will be used in a little less than 14 percent each.

Multiply the percentage required for each fabric by the total fabric required. For instance, multiply fifteen yards by 20 percent and you'll find you need to buy three yards each of the fabrics in that category. Multiply fifteen yards by one-third to find out how much of the fabric used the most you will need—five yards. Continue to calculate all yardage requirements, but figure border yardages separately.

Get Linked

There are many articles on my About.com Quilting Web site that will help you design a quilt. Here are few places to look first.

HOW TO DESIGN A QUILT

The place to find quilt design resources from around the Internet. You'll find lots of patterns to keep you busy and help you learn to make a quilt.

http://about.com/quilting/designresources

QUILTING GLOSSARY

My quilting glossary can help any time you're stumped by a new term. If you don't see a term, ask—my e-mail address is included on the Web site.

http://about.com/quilting/glossary

PLEASE RESCUE THIS UGLY QUILT

The layout isn't bad, but it could be better. Take a look at a quilt I call What Was I Thinking? and decide how you can improve it. The pattern is included.

http://about.com/quilting/rescuethisquilt

Chapter 4

Design and Sew Quilt Sashing and Borders

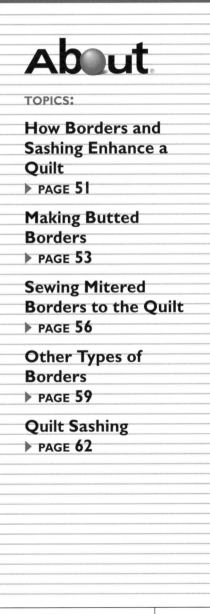

How Borders and Sashing Enhance a Quilt

Quilt borders are like picture frames. They surround the edges of a quilt and enhance its appearance. Sashing does the same thing for individual blocks. I nearly always choose my border fabrics after the quilt is assembled, because it's so much easier to select the perfect border fabrics after all of the other design elements are in place. That sometimes means I take the quilt top to a fabric shop, where I can stretch out long yardages of fabric right next to it—and where I'll get plenty of advice from staff and other quilters.

Wide borders can provide open areas where you can show off your quilting stitches. Multiple borders add adornment all by themselves. Borders can be mitered, with angled edges that meet at corners, or they can be sewn from straight-ended strips that butt against each other. Pieced borders can be simple or complex and add lots of visual appeal to the piece. Borders also play an important

How many borders should I use, and how wide should they be?

▶ The ideal number of borders varies. I like to use at least two, and often opt for three borders. I sometimes start with a dark, narrow inner border because I think it helps establish a frame for the quilt. Then I sew on a wider border that's between two-thirds and three-fourths the width of the quilt blocks. I sometimes finish with another narrow border. Experimentation is the best way to discover what works best for you and your quilts.

part in the final assembly of your quilt, because they help you square up sides that are sometimes skewed from handling.

Quilt sashings are design elements that are sewn between blocks within the interior of a quilt. Like borders, sashing can be plain or pieced. Sashing is often constructed to make blocks appear to link together, forming a secondary pattern that adds movement across the surface of the quilt. You'll find border and sashing instructions and design ideas throughout this chapter. Experiment a little the next time you make a quilt. You'll soon feel confident to design borders and sashing from scratch and make changes to quilting patterns, tailoring them to suit your own style.

Use these tips when you make long borders. Borders for miniature quilts and small wall hangings can usually be made from single lengths of fabric cut along the fabric's crosswise grain—from selvage to selvage. Fabric widths vary, but crosswise strips are typically anywhere from 40"– 43" long after prewashing and removing the unusable selvage.

You can also cut strips along the fabric's lengthwise grain, which runs parallel to the selvages. Lengthwise-grain strips are much less stretchy than crosswise strips, so they make excellent stabilizers for the sides of your quilt. But if you're making a bed-size quilt, its side borders could easily measure over 100" long, or nearly three yards. That's quite a bit of fabric to buy just for the border. Unless quilters are using large amounts of the same fabric throughout the quilt, we often piece together crosswise strips to achieve border length.

Whether or not to piece borders from short strips is a judgment call. Is your border fabric an intricate print that might be hard to match at seam intersections? If it is you might want to buy more yardage and use lengthwise-grain cuts. Long strips of fabric are sometimes the best choice for borders made from light solid fabrics, because seams where light fabrics are pieced together are often very noticeable.

To piece borders from crosswise strips, first use the measuring instructions for butted borders on the following pages to determine how long the borders should be. Remove selvages as you square up each end of a strip. Determine how many strips you need to achieve the right length and sew them together end to end with a ¼" seam allowance. Press seams open to reduce bulk. Trim back to the exact length if necessary.

Making Butted Borders

Butted borders, sometimes called straight-sewn borders, have ends that are cut straight across the fabric. Many quilters think they are the easiest type of border to sew on a quilt, but that doesn't mean they have to be boring. Repeat a fabric you've already used in the quilt to help unify and tie the design together, or choose something totally different to introduce an entirely new element to the project.

One of the most common mistakes new quilters make is to measure and cut border strips that match lengths along the outer perimeter of the quilt. What if the sides of the quilt that should match are different lengths? That's not unusual and occurs quite often because blocks sometimes stretch as we handle them during quilt assembly. If you sew mismatched borders to an uneven quilt it will compound the inaccuracy, making the quilt appear to be even more skewed. There's a simple—and easy—solution to the problem, one that gives you the opportunity to square up the quilt before you finish it.

Learn how to measure borders and use them to stabilize and square up a quilt. We'll use an easy technique to measure border lengths, then match and sew them to the quilt. The end result will be a quilt that's squared up and ready to finish. The

▸ A design wall helps you audition borders by placing lengths of fabric alongside your quilt. Design walls are sold commercially as thin, battinglike mats that unroll and can be tacked easily on the wall. The surface of the mat adheres to fabrics, and even smaller units will stick to it with no pinning. As mentioned earlier, you can also create a hanging design wall by sewing flannel yardage side-by-side until you reach the desired width.

step-by-step directions explain how to add butted side borders first, then top and bottom borders, but it's fine to start with the top and bottom pair if you prefer.

If you have a quilt that needs a border in order to square it up, follow these steps:

▶ Have a sharp pair of scissors on hand any time you plan to cut long borders. Sometimes it's easier and more accurate to use a pencil and your rotary cutting ruler to mark lengthwise-grain borders on the fabric before cutting them out with scissors. If you make a mistake with your rotary cutter the entire border might be ruined. If you make a mistake with a marker you have the opportunity to correct it before the border is cut.

1. Measure the quilt from top to bottom through its vertical midpoint.

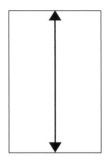

Fig. 4-1 **Measure the quilt's vertical midpoint**

2. Cut or piece two strips that match the length measured in step 1.
3. Fold one of the borders in half crosswise, wrong sides together. Finger crease at the fold. Fold the quilt crosswise, right sides together, to find the midpoint along one side.
4. Match the midpoint crease of the border to the midpoint crease of the quilt. The folds should nest into each other for an easy match. Pin the border to the quilt at the fold.
5. Match and pin the ends of the border to the ends of the quilt. Be sure to align all edges carefully. Match and pin the border to the remaining portion of the quilt sides, using your fingers to manipulate and distribute fullness if necessary—a process called **easing in**. Pin closely where you must ease in.

6. Sew the border to the quilt with a ¼" seam allowance. If you had to ease in fullness a great deal, place the longer of the two units against the **feed dogs**. Their gripping motion helps to distribute fullness. Press the seam allowance toward the border.

7. Repeat to sew a border to the opposite side of the quilt.

8. Measure the quilt through its horizontal midpoint to determine the length of top and bottom borders. Include the width of the side borders you just added. Cut or piece two borders to match that length.

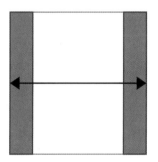

Fig. 4-2 **Measure the quilt's horizontal midpoint**

9. Fold the border in half and crease, just as you did for the side borders. Fold the quilt in half vertically to find its midpoint. Match and pin the midpoints at the top edge of the quilt, then match and pin the ends of the border to the left and right sides of the quilt.

10. Continue matching and pinning the border to the top of the quilt. Sew together with a ¼" seam allowance. Press the seam allowance toward the border. Repeat to add the bottom border.

11. Sew on additional butted borders using the same method.

WHAT'S HOT

▶ Some quilters feel that seams between pieced border strips are less noticeable when the strips are sewn together with a diagonal seam. I think the method you choose depends on the fabric and how easy it is to match the print along the diagonal. A diagonal seam that's noticeably off is more apparent than a well matched straight seam. You can sew borders together with diagonal seams using the technique for making long binding strips in Chapter 9.

Borders with corner squares are a variation of butted borders. The squares are often called corner blocks, corner squares, or cornerstones. They can be made from pieced or appliqué blocks or from squares of fabric.

Here is how to make a butted border with square ends:

1. Choose a border width. Add ½" to allow for two seam allowances. If you plan to use pieced blocks at the corners, the border width should match the unfinished width of the block. Measure the quilt both directions as you did for butted borders. Measure the top only; do not include width for borders.
2. Cut or piece two border strips for each length determined in step 1. If the ends of multiple borders will touch corner blocks, cut them now too, allowing a total of ½" for seam allowances where they will butt up against corner squares.
3. Sew strips for multiple-fabric borders side by side. Press seam allowances either direction.
4. Sew the side borders to the quilt using the same measure and match technique used for butted borders. Press seam allowances toward the border.
5. Sew corner squares to the ends of the top and bottom borders. Press seam allowances toward the border.
6. Sew the top and bottom borders to the quilt using the same measure and match technique used for side borders. Be sure to match seams where corner squares meet the inner seam of side borders. Press seam allowances toward the borders.

Sewing Mitered Borders to the Quilt

Mitered borders are joined at their ends with a diagonal seam. They can be used for any quilt borders and are an excellent choice

TOOLS YOU NEED

▶ Good rotary cutting skills are important when it's time to cut straight borders. Make sure your cutter is equipped with a sharp blade, and practice keeping the ruler steady as you cut. One tool that helps me rotary cut with absolutely no ruler slippage is the RuleSteady, a device that straddles the ruler and the rotary mat. The ruler is held firmly in place, allowing you to make perfect cuts every time.

for borders made from directional print fabrics, such as stripes, since the angled corners would allow stripes to flow in a continuous stream around the quilt.

Here is how to add a mitered border to a quilt:

1. Measure the quilt in both directions as you did to make butted borders. You're measuring the quilt only, not the width of planned borders.
2. Add twice the finished border width plus 4" to each measurement. Cut or piece two borders for each length—a pair for the sides and a pair for the top and bottom.
3. Cut or piece additional strips of the same length if you plan to add multiple borders. Sew borders for each side together lengthwise with a ¼" seam allowance. Press seam allowances in side borders toward the outer borders. Press seam allowances in top and bottom borders toward the inner border strips.
4. Fold a side border in half crosswise to find its midpoint. Mark the spot with a pin on the innermost border strip. Divide the original vertical length of the quilt by two. Measure outward on each side of the pin, stopping at that distance from the center. Pencil-mark both spots along the edge of the innermost border strip.
5. Place the 45-degree line of a rotary ruler against one end of the strip, on its reverse side and with the side of the ruler on the mark and angled toward the end of the strip. Draw an angled line alongside the ruler to represent your seam line.
6. Draw a second angled line parallel to and ¼" past the first. The new line is your cutting line, but do not cut just yet.
7. Repeat to mark lines on the opposite end of the strip, then measure and mark the top and bottom borders using the same techniques.

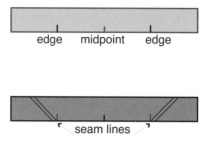

Fig. 4-3 Marking match points and miters

I want to use a striped fabric as my border. Do I need to use a different cutting method?

▸ Directional prints, like plaids and stripes, are attractive in borders. They add an element of movement to the quilt design and can become a focal point. Sometimes directionals are not printed in sync with the fabric grain, so cutting along grain lines does not result in a straight design. If that's not the look you want, cut directionals along pattern lines instead. Handle the strips carefully to avoid stretch, since cuts will probably be along the bias.

8. Align a side border to the edge of the quilt, matching and pinning mid- and endpoints as you did for butted borders. Align and pin the remaining areas of the border to the quilt.
9. Sew the border to the quilt from marked endpoint to the opposite marked endpoint. Do not sew into the area reserved for seam allowances. **Backstitch** at the beginning and end of the seam.
10. Repeat steps 8 and 9 to pin and sew all borders to the quilt.
11. Fold borders carefully at corners, diagonally and right sides together, matching and pinning along the marked diagonal lines. Be sure to match the seam intersections for multiple borders.
12. Sew one corner together, beginning at the spot where side seams ended. Backstitch at the beginning of the seam and sew all the way to the end of the patches. Repeat to connect the borders in remaining corners.
13. Inspect the front of the quilt to make sure miters are sewn correctly at corners. If they look good, trim away excess border lengths along the marked cutting lines. Press seam allowances open.

Other Types of Borders

You've read how to make borders from one or more strips of fabric, but there's no limit to the layout designs you can create with borders. Patchwork borders are an excellent way to help you extend the design within your quilt to its outer edges. Use them alone or in combination with plain strips of fabric. Appliqué borders look wonderful with both patchwork and appliqué quilts and give you the opportunity to incorporate softly rounded designs into an otherwise angular layout.

Let's look at a few easy ways to make patchwork borders. Patchwork borders are also called pieced borders. They can be very intricate, but sometimes a simple patchwork strip is all it takes to highlight the interior of your quilt and make it look stunning. Most of these borders can be quick pieced or strip pieced, saving time and letting you see the results quickly.

Half-square triangles are a popular quilting component and are often used to create pieced borders. They are easy to make and can be arranged in numerous ways to change their appearance. You can learn to make quick pieced, half-square triangles by following the instructions in Chapter 7.

WHAT'S HOT

▶ You'll find plenty of inspiration for borders and other design elements by attending quilt shows and looking at quilts online. Our About.com Quilts for Kids Gallery is an online display of quilts made by members of our forums. Be sure to take a look at the gallery the next time you're online. There you'll find examples of many types of borders incorporated into the quilt designs. Visit http://about.com/quilting/forkids.

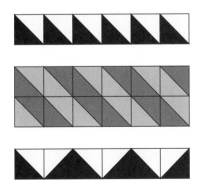

Fig. 4-4 **Three ways to make borders from half-square triangles**

Flying Geese units are used to make directional borders. They can be quickly pieced and strung together to make any border length you choose.

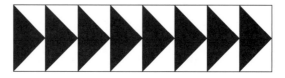

Fig. 4-5 Flying Geese border

Any other type of piecing method can be used for borders. Try checkerboards, a continuous string of squares in alternating colors. Or try making small nine-patch blocks. You'll learn to make string-pieced blocks in Chapter 11, but the technique can also be used to create borders.

Take a little time to determine the best size for your patchwork border components. Measure your quilt for patchwork borders using the same technique used to measure a quilt for borders with corner squares, then find the finished length of borders by deducting ½" to compensate for the ending seam allowances on each side. What number will divide evenly into the finished size of the border? For instance, if your quilt top's finished size is 60" square you can use 3" units to assemble borders because 60 divided by 3 equals 20. You have lots of choices for unit size because 6, 2, and 2½ also divide evenly into 60".

If your quilt is rectangular you'll need to find a unit size that works for the side borders and the top and bottom borders. That can be a little trickier, but it is usually doable. There are a few techniques that should help you add pieced borders to any quilt:

ELSEWHERE ON THE WEB

▶ Womenfolk.com gives us quite a few articles about quilting history. One of my favorite pages focuses on multiple borders used in medallion quilts—quilts with a focal center that are typically surrounded by rows of borders. As they radiate outward, borders in historical medallion quilts are often very different, combining plain borders with pieced and appliqué examples. This page includes photos of vintage quilts and a few techniques to help you make your own medallion quilt: www.women folk.com/quilting_history/medallion.htm.

- If you know in advance that you want to use a pieced border, tailor your layout to produce a quilt with sides that can be evenly divided by three or four, which are commonly used component sizes.
- Alter the dimensions of your quilt by sewing on a plain inner border first, cutting it to a width that will make the side dimensions work with pieced units. Determine the finished size of the filler border first, then add ½" for side seam allowances.
- If nothing seems to work, consider adding a string-pieced border, which is made up of randomly sized strips and can be cut to any length you desire.

You could finish your quilt with an appliqué border. With appliqué borders there's no worry about making units that precisely match the side of the quilt. Measure and cut butted or mitered borders from panels of fabric and sew them to the quilt. Arrange your appliqué motifs on the borders and appliqué them to the fabric using your favorite technique. Read about appliqué methods in Chapter 5.

Try using a special border print in your quilts. Special border fabrics are designed with a series of narrow to wide stripes that are printed side by side and run along the length of the fabric. Stripes are usually repeated two or more times across the fabric's width, giving you the opportunity to piece them together at match points in order to create longer stripes with shorter yardages.

The stripes in any one border-print fabric coordinate with each other, and that makes it easy to create attractive multiborder quilts. Try using one of the wider stripes for a quilt's most prominent

WHAT'S HOT

▶ Even perfect borders can become rippled and stretched along their outer edges when you quilt the quilt. To eliminate rippling, hand-sew long stitches, called basting stitches, close to the outer edge of problem borders. Pull gently on both ends of the thread to distribute and minimize ripples. Measure the sides of the quilt to make sure you've solved the problem. Bind the quilt, allowing the binding to cover the basting stitches. Refer to Chapter 9 for binding instructions.

border, add a plain border around it, and then finish with a narrower stripe around the quilt's outer edges.

There's often no need to mark quilting designs on a border-print stripe—simply quilt around some of the motifs in the design. Border prints are nearly always part of a larger collection of fabrics, so you can usually choose from several coordinating prints when you design the quilt.

Quilt Sashing

The most commonly used sashing is made from plain bars of fabric sewn between blocks in a quilt, but sashing can be as varied as borders. You can make sashing from pieced units or from strips with appliqué motifs sewn to them. Corner squares can be used at the ends of sashing just as they are in borders.

Fig. 4-6 **Plain sashing and pieced sashing**

Plain sashing should be cut to a length that equals the finished length of the block size it will be sewn next to plus ½" to allow for seam allowances. Width is up to you. Pieced sashing should be planned just like pieced borders so that it fits correctly along the sides of your blocks. Try using a border print in your sashing—it's an easy way to create an intricate looking sashing by simply cutting strips of fabric.

Sashing can help you square up skewed blocks just like borders can, but you'll have best results if you make blocks carefully so that the sashing fits without a struggle. Match and pin sashing midpoints to the block first, then ends. Finish by matching and pinning sashing along the entire length of the block, then sew.

WHAT'S HOT

▶ You'll find instructions to help you make Flying Geese on my Quilting Web site, where I cover a few different assembly methods (http://about.com/quilting/flying geese). One of my wall hangings is made with a series of Flying Geese borders combined with borders made from a floral border print fabric. The quilt is called Which Way Do We Go? You'll find instructions for it online at http://about.com/quilting/whichway.

Get Linked

Here are a few patterns from my Web site for quilts that are made with pieced borders and sashing.

STRETCHING TO THE STARS

Star quilts are always popular, and this one is quick and easy to assemble. Two sizes of star blocks are surrounded by pieced sashing that continues into the quilt's borders.

http://about.com/quilting/stretchingtothestars

WALK AROUND THE BLOCK

You can assemble this little miniature quilt in a day. Three borders and small pieced blocks surround a center medallion that's cut from a pictorial fabric. A narrow border separates two wider borders.

http://about.com/quilting/walkaroundtheblock

CATCHING THE VIEW

Three curious cats are sitting in watercolor style windows that are surrounded by mitered frames.

http://about.com/quilting/catchingtheview

Chapter 5

Appliqué Methods

Introduction to Appliqué

Appliqué is the art of sewing pieces of fabric onto a larger background. Appliqué has the reputation of being difficult, but there are so many different forms of the technique to choose from that I'm sure you'll find a method that's easy to accomplish on your very first try. Some types of hand appliqué do take a bit of practice, but the results are so rewarding that once you have the technique down pat you'll be hooked—and off to create your next appliqué quilt.

Let's talk about some of the tools required to create an appliqué quilt, get a jump start on the terms you'll hear in patterns, and cover a few important techniques that will help you create all types of appliqué.

You may already own the most important appliqué tools, but there are a few special tools that will help you complete your appliqué projects more easily, with fewer snags along the way. There's no need to rush out and buy them all before you begin. Use what

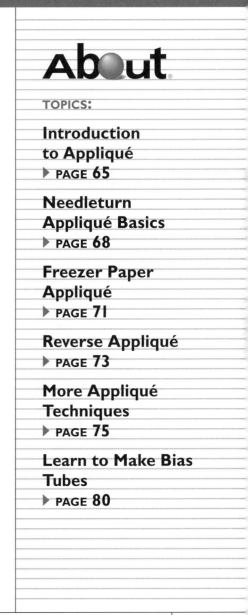

About®

you have on hand and add specialty products as you discover which types of appliqué are your favorites.

Scissors
- Special appliqué scissors are usually small with very sharp blades that cut all the way to their tips.
- Another type of appliqué scissors has angled controls and a paddle-shaped blade on the bottom. When you trim fabric edges, the paddle blade pushes the seam allowance fabric out of the way a bit as it makes the cut. That action helps keep you from cutting too close to the fold line.

Needles
- Quilters like to use long, thin needles for their hand appliqué. Look for needles labeled sharps, straw, or milliner's.
- For machine appliqué, choose a thin needle size, such as 60/8.

Appliqué Threads
- For hand appliqué, choose fine cotton thread that matches or blends with your motifs. The better the blend, the more it will disappear into the sides of your work.
- Use machine embroidery thread when you do decorative machine appliqué.
- Very fine transparent nylon thread can be used for blind machine appliqué, where you want stitches to be invisible. Some quilters do not think it is a good choice for heirloom projects. If you do use nylon thread, be sure to choose types that are finer than a strand of hair—not thread that resembles fishing line.

TOOLS YOU NEED

▶ Many manufacturers make excellent scissors, but my personal favorite is Gingher. The company makes just about any type of scissors you need for any sewing task, including appliqué scissors with a special paddle blade to protect your work when you trim seam allowances. Visit www.gingher.com and click on Product Catalog from the top menu, then select Sewing and Craft Scissors from the menu on the left and then Appliqué Scissors from the drop-down menu on the left.

Template Materials

- Appliqué patterns are turned into templates, which are rigid reproductions of the pattern. To make a template, first use a photocopier or scanner to copy the image. Next print the shape and glue it onto cardboard or special template plastic, then cut out. Another option is to place template plastic over full-size images and trace them onto the plastic, then cut. Make a template for each shape in your project. Appliqué templates do not include seam allowances.

Prepare your background fabric for appliqué. Most appliqué quilts are made from individual blocks that are sewn together to make a quilt top—just like patchwork quilts. Instead of piecing small patches together, you'll arrange and sew shapes onto plain pieces of fabric.

Here is how to prep your background fabric for appliqué:

1. Cut a background piece that's about 1" longer and wider than its finished dimensions. Backgrounds sometimes become skewed a bit as we sew shapes to them. The generous size makes it easy to square up the block before it is sewn into the quilt.
2. Fold the background along each diagonal and finger press. Fold it vertically and horizontally and finger press along each fold. The fold lines make evenly spaced areas of the block more visible and help you arrange shapes accurately.
3. For simple layouts, the fold lines are all you'll need to arrange patches. If your layout is complex, make a full size copy of it and center the fabric on top of the copy. Place it on top of a light box or tape the two to a window—back-lighting makes the pattern visible through the fabric. Use a

pencil or disappearing marker to lightly trace the pattern onto the fabric.

Use these tips to work with curved shapes. Working with curves isn't difficult at all, but there are a few things you can do to make it even easier. Curves that stretch inward are called concave curves. Their edges fold under more easily when you make small inward clips in the seam allowance with your sharp scissors. Curves that bend outwards, called convex curves, do not need to be clipped.

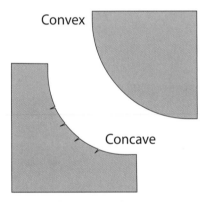

Fig. 5-1 Concave and convex curves

Needleturn Appliqué Basics

Needleturn appliqué is the traditional appliqué method. In needleturn appliqué you cut out each fabric shape and pin it to the background fabric. There's no need to turn under seam allowances ahead of time—they're coaxed under with the needle as you sew.

Here is how to appliqué using the needleturn method:

1. Make templates for shapes in your project. If some shapes appear as mirror images there's no need to make two templates. Simply flip the single template upside down to make a mirror-image shape.

2. Place a template right-side up on fabric and trace around its edges. Cut out the shape, adding an approximate $\frac{3}{16}$" seam allowance. Clip inner curves if necessary. Repeat to cut out all shapes required for the quilt block.

3. Pin your fabric shapes to the background block, starting with pieces on the bottom layer and moving forward. Pin shapes in place or use large basting stitches to keep them from shifting. You won't need to appliqué edges that lie behind other patches, but some quilters keep them secure by sewing them to the background with a quick running stitch.

4. Select thread that matches the patch you'll sew first. Thread the needle with about 15" to 20" of the thread and knot one end. You'll sew with one strand of thread.

5. Guide the needle through the back of the block, making it emerge just inside the marked line on the first piece. Begin sewing patches positioned at the rear of the design.

6. Fold under the first bit of seam allowance with the tip of the needle, making sure the marked line is under the fold.

7. Use the fingers of your free hand to hold the fold in place and insert the needle into the background fabric next to the spot where it first emerged. Keep a fluid motion going by moving the tip of the needle up from behind the background, allowing it to catch a few threads on the side of the fold.

8. Pull the thread to its full length and tug lightly. The stitches should seem to melt into the background and sides of the

ELSEWHERE ON THE WEB

▶ The Appliqué Society is a group that promotes the teaching and appreciation of appliqué. They sponsor an annual show and keep their members up to date on appliqué news and techniques. If you're interested in joining, visit the Web site for more information at www .theappliquesociety.org.

► Sometimes the long pins we use for patchwork are too cumbersome to use in our appliqué projects. They stick out and prick us while we're trying to sew, and our hand sewing thread gets wrapped around their heads or sharp ends. Sequin pins are a good alternative. They are thin and about a half-inch long, short enough to keep them from getting in the way while you sew. Most quilt shops, fabric stores, and craft stores sell sequin pins.

piece. Continue folding and sewing until you've sewn the entire patch to the background. Experiment a bit to discover how many stitches you can take before pulling the thread to its entire length.

9. At the ending stitch, insert the needle through the background and make a small stitch behind the patch. Instead of pulling the thread taut, leave a loop. Guide the needle through the loop and pull to create a knot. Clip the excess fabric.

10. Appliqué all remaining pieces to the background. Place the block under a square ruler and square it up to measure ½" more than its finished size.

Use these tips to polish your needleturn appliqué skills. Needleturn appliqué isn't difficult once you've had a little practice, but there are a few methods that will get you off to a quick start. Try these techniques—but don't be afraid to experiment to find your very own special methods.

Points can get bulky when you fold under the seam allowances on their sides, but you can use a few tricks to make them more cooperative. When you sew an outside point, like the tip of a triangle, stop a stitch or two before the point end and trim away excess point fabric that you've folded under along the first edge. Clip off the top of the point just a bit, then fold under the first section of the opposite side of the point. Continue sewing around the point.

Inside points require a different method. Think of the inner point where the sides of a star meet. Use your scissors to clip the inside point to the seam allowance. Stop sewing a stitch or so before you reach the point and turn under the seam allowance on the next side. Stitch again, bringing the needle up a few threads inward from the point. Place the needle through the patch and background again directly on the point, then continue sewing the next side of the shape.

If you have a difficult time using the needle to turn fabric, try turning it under with a toothpick. Right-handed sewers usually find that it's easier to hand appliqué in a counterclockwise direction. Left-handed sewers will sew clockwise.

Some quilters like to turn under patch edges before they sew. You might find that turning under edges as you sew just isn't your favorite technique. That's okay, because you can turn them under first and use the same stitch to sew pieces to the background.

Heat-resistant templates will help you manage seams. The material resembles plastic but will not melt when you touch it with an iron. Cut out your patches as you would for needleturn appliqué, leaving an approximate ³⁄₁₆" seam allowance. Go ahead and clip curves and prepare points. Spray a bit of spray starch into a small cup and grab a few cotton swaps from the medicine cabinet. Place the fabric wrong-side up on your ironing board and center the template on top of it. Soak up a bit of starch with a cotton swab and dampen a short distance of seam allowance. Use a hot iron to force the seam allowance up over the template. Continue swabbing and pressing until you've pressed all seams under. Arrange pressed pieces on your background and appliqué them in place.

Freezer Paper Appliqué

There are a few different ways to use freezer paper for appliqué. Freezer paper has a plain paper side and a side that appears to be coated with a thin layer of plastic. The shiny, plastic-like side sticks to fabric when you touch it with an iron. You can buy freezer paper at the grocery store (in the same aisle as the foil and plastic wrap), but quilting tool manufacturers have developed freezer paper with

ELSEWHERE ON THE WEB

▶ Piece O' Cake Designs is a company established by two seasoned appliqué artists, Becky Goldsmith and Linda Jenkins. The pair have written numerous books about the art of appliqué, and they also provide helpful advice and patterns on their Web site. Click through to their Notions page to read descriptions of some of their favorite tools. They specialize in appliqué, so you can't go wrong with their recommendations. Visit www.pieceo cake.com.

I have a hard time manipulating my big iron to turn under tiny seams. Is there an easy way to do it?

▶ I agree. Standard size irons are difficult to twist and turn onto seam allowances of small patches. Browse some of the online resources listed in the appendix and you'll find a variety of mini irons— I think of them as irons on a stick. They have small pressing heads that are mounted to a pen-sized handle and are so much easier to manipulate than a large iron.

gridded lines that help us arrange and cut patches. The paper sold in quilt shops also seems to stick to fabric a bit better than traditional freezer paper.

This is my favorite way to appliqué using freezer paper:

1. Place an appliqué template right-side up on the paper side of freezer paper and trace around it. Cut out. Repeat to make the total number of shapes required for your project.
2. Press the plastic-like side of each shape to the front side of fabric. Cut out, leaving an approximate ³⁄₁₆" seam allowance around the edges of each paper shape.
3. Peel off the freezer paper and center it on the reverse side of the fabric, but this time place the shiny, plastic-like side up. Secure the paper to the patch with a straight pin.
4. Trim points and clip curves if necessary. Repeat for all pieces in your design.
5. Use a mini iron or the tip of your regular iron to press the seam allowance over the edges of the freezer paper. The fabric will stick to the paper.
6. Position the pieces on the background, working from back to front in the design. Sew the pieces to the background just as you would for needleturn appliqué. Stop sewing a short distance from the beginning of your seam and remove the freezer paper. The starched seam should refold easily so that you can finish sewing the piece to the background.
7. Tie off threads as you would for needleturn appliqué. Square up the background when all patches are in place.

Some quilters leave the freezer paper in place until all patches are sewn to the background. They turn the piece over and make small slits into the background fabric—just enough to reach in with tweezers and pull out the freezer paper.

It's easy to pull the paper out from under pieces with edges that are covered by another shape. Just reach in through the unsewn edge and remove the paper before sewing a patch on top of that side.

Learn to make sharp points when you do freezer paper appliqué. For inside points, clip the fabric to the seam line like you did for the needleturn method. Press edges onto the freezer paper. If you're working with outside points, fold the seam allowance straight down, making the top of the fold even with the point. Press one side edge onto the freezer paper. Press the remaining edge onto the paper carefully, checking to make sure the point is nice and neat.

TOOLS YOU NEED

▶ There are an ever-growing number of specialty tools to help you appliqué. I find that a heat-resistant finger protector keeps me from burning myself when I'm trying to fold under seam allowances with an iron. It slips over your finger like a partial glove, keeping you cool even if the iron bumps into it.

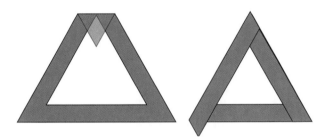

Fig. 5-2 **Folding sharp points onto freezer paper**

Reverse Appliqué

For reverse appliqué, you'll cut shapes within your appliqué motifs. The edges of the holes are turned under to expose another layer of fabric beneath the patch. The fabric that peeks through the little windows can be your background fabric, but it's more popular to insert another fabric underneath the motif. Mark all design lines on your template. It might be necessary to cut out the inner lines with a razor knife—scissors usually aren't too easy to manipulate within small edges.

Here is how to reverse appliqué:

1. Position your template right-side up on the right side of your fabric. Mark the fold line around the exterior of the template and mark around all of the openings within its interior.
2. Cut the shape out, leaving an approximate ³⁄₁₆" seam allowance around the exterior fold line. Clip inside curves and points if necessary.
3. Use sharp scissors to cut slits at the center of shapes on the interior of the patch.
4. Trace around the template on the right side of the fabric you plan to place under the motif. Cut out on the line—no seam allowance is necessary.
5. Center the background piece right-side up over the front piece, also right-side up, placing it within the top piece's fold lines. Use a straight pin through both layers to keep the pieces from shifting.

Fig. 5-3 **Assembling reverse appliqué**

6. Appliqué the top piece to the background, sewing around its outer edges. Trim excess fabric from interior slits as needed to fold them under. Appliqué along the folds to expose the fabric underneath.

More Appliqué Techniques

There are many more ways to appliqué shapes to a background fabric. A few are described here, but be on the lookout for other ideas. Quilters are constantly developing new tools and techniques to make appliqué easier and more accurate, helping eliminate the notion that appliqué is difficult.

Try sew-and-turn appliqué the next time you want to make a quick project. Here's an easy appliqué method that lets you prepare pieces without folding under their edges. Two appliqué shapes are sewn together along their edges, right sides together, then turned inside out before sewing. This method works best with simple shapes. Seam allowances can get a bit messy at turns if shapes are intricate or steeply angled.

Use fabric for both layers if you would like a little three-dimension depth to your shapes. For a sheer look, cut the backing from nonwoven interfacing or from used clothes dryer softener sheets.

Follow these steps to try sew-and-turn appliqué:

1. Place your appliqué template right-side down on the reverse side of the fabric that will be face up in your design. Trace around the shape. Trace more shapes as needed, leaving about ½" between them.
2. Place the backing fabric under the marked fabric, right sides together. Machine sew on each line, going past the beginning stitches a bit when you come around to the seam's starting point. Repeat for all shapes.
3. Cut through both layers, leaving an approximate ³⁄₁₆" seam allowance around all edges. Clip inside corners if necessary, and trim bulky fabric from points.
4. Make a short slit in the reverse side of the shape, just enough to reach in and turn the fabrics right-side out. Run a point

TOOLS YOU NEED

▶ J.T. Trading offers a product called 505 Spray and Fix. It's a temporary adhesive that can be used for many purposes, including appliqué and machine embroidery. Pieces are repositionable and the product is odorless and colorless. It won't gum up your sewing needles. It's also a good choice for temporary basting. You can read more about 505 Spray and Fix on the company's Web site at www.sprayandfix.com/505.html.

turner or other dull instrument, like the cover of a ball point pen, around the inside of the patch to smooth out its edges. Repeat for other patches.

5. Press all patches and appliqué them to the background.

Quick-fuse appliqué is the fastest method of all. This easy appliqué technique is done with a product called fusible web. You won't have to turn under the edges of the shapes—just sew around them with a decorative hand or machine stitch. Fusing is quick, so you get to see your project in no time at all.

Fusible web has a paper-backed side and a side with a sheer web-like appearance. The webbed side is pressed onto the reverse side of fabric, where it quickly adheres. The paper side is then removed to expose the other side of the webbing. Patches are placed onto the background, webbing side down, and pressed in place.

Here is how to use quick-fuse appliqué:

1. Place your template right-side down on the paper side of fusible web. Mark around it. Repeat if you need more identical shapes. Place the images close together because no seam allowance is necessary.
2. Continue marking shapes, grouping pieces together if you need multiple pieces from the same fabric.
3. Cut the marked fusible web apart in sections, leaving shapes together if they're to be cut from identical fabric.
4. Place one group of shapes on the reverse side of fabric, paper-side up. Follow manufacturer's recommendations to fuse the web in place.
5. Cut each shape out on the marked line. Remove the paper layer from all shapes and position them on your background, moving from rear to front in the design. Fuse all shapes in place at the same time.

WHAT'S HOT

▶ Try raw-edged appliqué for a casual look. Baste or pin fabric shapes to the background and machine sew around their edges, leaving ¼" or more of fabric past the seam. Try sewing with a straight line or a zigzag line, and use any type of thread you wish, matching or contrasting. You can either leave the raw edges as is or snip them a bit with scissors to encourage fraying. It's fine to use hand stitches for projects that won't be washed as often, such as miniatures and wall hangings.

6. Finish the edges of fabric patches by sewing around them with a decorative hand or machine stitch, such as the blanket stitch.
7. Square up the block as needed.

Sew a blanket stitch around your patch edges. Sewing a blanket stitch around your fused shapes is an easy way to finish the edges in a decorative way. Thread an embroidery needle with one or two strands of embroidery floss and knot one end. Starting on the reverse side, bring the needle through the background fabric at point A, right along the edge of a fused shape (see image below). Hold the thread down with your thumb and circle it in a counterclockwise direction, piercing the fabric with needle at point B. Bring the needle back through the fabric at point C—even with and across from A. Keep the loop of the thread under the needle. Pull the thread and repeat to make more stitches.

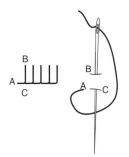

Fig. 5-4 Learn to sew the blanket stitch

There are many ways to appliqué by machine. A few of my favorite machine appliqué techniques are described in this chapter. Machine stitching takes place quickly, and stitches can be difficult to remove to make corrections, so be sure to practice these techniques on scraps of fabric before you attempt to use them in your projects. No matter which machine appliqué method you use, bring the bobbin thread to the front before you begin sewing. To do that, grab the top thread and take one stitch, stopping with the needle up. If your machine can't easily take just one stitch, turn the flywheel manually. After taking the stitch, tug on the top thread to pull the bobbin thread up through the fabric. This step keeps the bobbin thread from becoming entangled underneath your work.

Here's how to do straight stitch machine appliqué:

1. Thread a thin sewing machine needle with thread.
2. Turn under the seam allowance of the rear appliqué shape and pin the shape to your background fabric. Take a stitch near the edge of the patch and pull the bobbin thread to the front of the block. Sew several stitches at 0 length to anchor the seam and gradually increase stitch length until you are sewing about twelve stitches per inch—or longer stitches if you prefer.
2. Continue sewing around the shape. Begin decreasing the stitch length as you near the seam's starting point. Finish with a few stitches set at 0. Do not backstitch or overlap previous stitches.
3. If you must sew inner or outer points, stop with the needle down and lift the presser foot. Pivot the fabric to the next side of the shape and continue sewing.

You can also machine appliqué with a blind stitch—the same type of seam you use when you hem garments. Blind-stitch appliqué is the type of machine appliqué that most closely resembles hand appliqué. Turn under the edges of your shapes before you begin and use a very fine nylon thread through the needle. Nylon is sometimes a problem when used in the bobbin, so try a cotton sewing thread in that position. Use clear nylon to sew light fabrics and smoke-colored nylon for darker patches.

Refer to your sewing machine owner's manual to set it up for a blind hem stitch. The stitch takes several small, straight stitches forward, then zigzags to the left before repeating its straight progression. Take several stitches on sample fabric so that you have a feel for the needle's actions.

Here is how to do blind-stitch machine appliqué:

1. Place the rear patch on the background and pin in place. You'll position and sew all patches from the rear of the design forwards.
2. Place the unit in the machine so that the straight stitches will enter the background fabric only and the zigzag will move over to catch the appliqué shape. Start on a straight edge or gentle curve if possible. Take a stitch and bring the bobbin thread to the top.
3. Stitch around the edges of the piece, ending the seam just past its starting point. Tie the bobbin thread to the top thread and trim the thread back to very near the knot. Repeat to add all other shapes to the background.

Satin stitching is another machine appliqué technique. It highlights the edges of your appliqué shapes. A satin stitch is a very closely spaced zigzag stitch. You can sew with matching thread that blends with your pieces or you can choose something that adds a burst of color for contrast. Use a tear-away stabilizer, available at discount stores and fabric shops, behind the background to eliminate puckers that sometimes occur with satin stitching. Machine embroidery thread works well for this technique.

ELSEWHERE ON THE WEB

▶ Mimi Dietrich is a wonderful teacher and you won't meet a nicer person. She knows how to explain appliqué from start to finish and can walk beginners through the process with ease. Her Web site always includes a free pattern, but it's worth a visit just to browse her online quilt gallery. You can even order autographed copies of books directly from Mimi. Visit www.mimidietrich .com.

Refer to your sewing machine manual to set up the machine to sew the satin stitch. Place the stabilizer on the back of sample fabric and experiment with stitch width before you work on the blocks.

Working forward in the design, surround all appliqué shapes with satin stitching, spacing stitch width so that half of it covers the edge of the shape and the other half is in the background fabric. There's no need to turn raw edges under because the stitches will protect them and hold them firmly in place.

Learn to Make Bias Tubes

Narrow bias tubes are flexible shapes that can be used to create appliqué flower stems, basket handles, and many other flowing shapes. They are also used for Celtic appliqué and to separate individual pieces in appliqué that mimics stained glass windows.

Bias bars are long, thin, heat-resistant flats that are sold in sets of different widths. They are used to press bias tubes neatly after assembly. You can make bias tubes without bias bars, but the results are usually less than spectacular. Look for bias tubes at fabric stores and quilt shops. They are available online from many fabric merchants.

Follow these steps to make a bias tube:

1. Determine how wide your bias tubes should be. Double the desired finished width and add ¾". Cut bias strips that length by placing the 45-degree line of a long rotary ruler at the bottom edge of fabric and cutting along the side of the ruler.
2. Fold strips lengthwise, wrong sides together. Sew a ¼" seam allowance along the lengthwise edge. Trim back the seam allowance, leaving at least ⅛".
3. Insert the press bar that corresponds with the tube's finished width into one end of the tube. Center the seam in

the middle of the bar and press it open. Spritz on a bit of water or spray starch if necessary to keep the seam flat. Move the bar along the length of the tube to press its entire length.

4. Remove the bar and press again if necessary. Cut the tube into required lengths and appliqué to the background. Since they are constructed from bias cuts, the tubes should arch gracefully around shapes.

Get Linked

You'll find more appliqué help on the About.com Quilting Web site. Use these resources to get started with an appliqué project today.

HAND APPLIQUÉ

Find information about many types of hand appliqué, including needleturn and traditional Hawaiian appliqué techniques.
http://about.com/quilting/handapplique

STAINED GLASS APPLIQUÉ INSTRUCTIONS

Learn traditional and quick ways to make stained glass appliqué, which resembles stained glass windows.
http://about.com/quilting/stainedglassapplique

MACHINE APPLIQUÉ TECHNIQUES

We talked about machine appliqué in this chapter, but you'll find lots of tips and instructions for more stitches online.
http://about.com/quilting/machineapplique

Chapter 6

Rotary Cutting Essentials

Introduction to Rotary Cutting

Quilters have developed thousands of timesaving tools and techniques over the years, and I rank rotary cutting right up there near the top of the heap in importance. Done correctly, rotary cutting helps you make a quilt in much less time and it enhances your accuracy. Forget about using templates to mark each patch of fabric and get ready to give your hands a much needed rest from scissors. You'll feel confident about rotary cutting after just a bit of practice—and ready to rotary cut pieces for all of your quilts. Rotary cutting is accomplished by placing a thick, see-through ruler on top of fabric to measure it and hold it in place. A rotary cutter, which looks a lot like a round-bladed pizza cutter, is rolled along the edge of the ruler to cut the fabric. All of your cutting takes place on a special rotary cutting mat that's designed to help grip the fabric and protect the surface of your cutting table from damage that would most certainly occur if a rotary cutter were rolled across it.

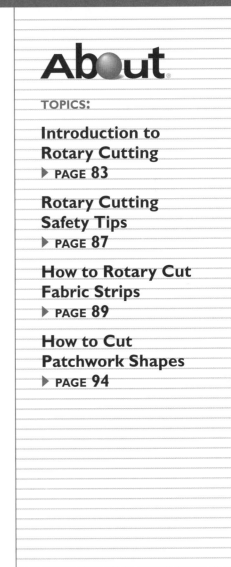

About

There are what seems like an endless number of rotary cutting tools to choose from, all with advantages and disadvantages. The information in this chapter will help you sort through the selections to find the best tools for your workspace.

You need a few basic tools to get started with rotary cutting: a rotary cutter, a 6" x 24" rotary ruler, and a special rotary cutting mat. Those three basic tools allow you to make the majority of cuts used in quilting. Hold off on buying additional rulers until you're accustomed to the rotary cutting process. Once you've made a few quilts you'll have a much better feel for which rulers you need.

You'll find a large variety of rotary cutters whether you shop online or off. A rotary cutter does look like a pizza cutter, but there's an important difference between the two. The rotary cutter's blade is razor sharp and will slice into just about anything it touches—including your fingers. A rotary blade has to be sharp in order to cut multiple layers of fabric over and over without becoming dull too quickly. Treat the cutter with respect and you won't need to wear bandages whenever you use it.

Some rotary cutters have perfectly straight handles and some are curved to fit your palm. Some have indentations in the handle to cushion your fingers. You'll find all types of rotary cutters online, but for your first purchase I think it's best to try several styles out in person to see how they fit your hand, especially if you have arthritis or another condition that makes it difficult to hold onto objects.

Rotary cutters all have some type of protective sheath to cover the blade. The blade cover on most rotary cutters is a manual device—usually something you click with your thumb or another finger when you want to open and close the cutter. Some styles of rotary cutters have blades that automatically engage when you press down on them to cut fabric. Either type can cut you if you aren't careful. If you brush your hand across an open-bladed cutter, you'll get nicked. Drop a pressure-sensitive cutter on top of your foot and it might hit hard enough to cut you.

Rotary cutters are equipped with different blade sizes. Small blades that measure 28 mm across are easily manipulated around curves. The midsized rotary blade measures 45 mm. It's an all-purpose blade that will handle all of your rotary cutting tasks. Cutters with a 60 mm blade are another option. They make it easy to slice through heavier fabrics or multiple layers of any fabric. I recommend that you start with a cutter that holds either a 45 mm or 60 mm blade.

Most rotary cutters can be configured for right-handed or left-handed use. A few cannot, so check the package description to make sure you purchase a cutter that works in your cutting hand.

I'm always amazed at the number of rotary rulers we can choose from. Rotary rulers are thick and transparent. They are designed so that a rotary cutter can slice down their length while butting snugly against their tallish sides to make a straight cut. The thickness serves another purpose—it helps keep the blade from accidentally going off track and skipping across the top of the ruler. That's important, because your fingers are on top of the ruler when you make a cut.

The only thing different brands of rotary rulers have in common is transparency. Every manufacturer uses a different color and width to mark ruler lines that are used to measure fabric. Most rulers are marked in ⅛" increments—you'll have to estimate any cut smaller.

Some rulers can be flipped over to reveal lines of a different color. The thin, dark lines of some rulers are highlighted by a bright color, such as yellow or orange. Most rulers have tiny openings placed strategically along rule lines to help you inspect fabric placement more closely before you make a cut.

I like several different brands of rulers, but all of my favorites have very thin rule lines, since wider lines make it more difficult to determine exactly where to place fabric edges when it's time to cut.

Your 6" x 24" rotary ruler should also have a series of angled lines that stretch across its width—a 30-degree line, a 45-degree line, and a 60-degree line. Later in the chapter you'll learn how to use the angled lines to cut different patchwork shapes.

If you want to add onto your collection with additional helpful rulers, consider these:

○ A 6½" square ruler marked in ⅛" increments and with a diagonal line from one corner to another helps you cut individual pieces of fabric. It's also useful for creating the popular half-square triangle units, where two triangles occupy each half of a pieced square.

○ A 12½" square ruler helps you make sure blocks are square and is also helpful when tidying up a quilt's corners after the quilting stitches are in place, because quilting sometimes distorts the edges of a quilt. The ruler also makes it easy to cut large squares of fabric for appliqué and other purposes.

○ A 15½" square ruler works in the same way as the smaller 12½" square ruler but helps you work with larger quilt blocks.

Choose a rotary mat that suits your work area. Rotary mats aren't quite as varied as rulers and cutters, but you do need to put a bit of thought into your selection. I always advise new quilters to buy the largest mat they can afford that also fits their workspaces, because larger mats make it much easier to position fabric when it's time to cut. A 24" x 35" mat is large enough to work with fabric folded once along its lengthwise grain into a bundle about 22" tall—a type of cut that's very common. If your workspace is too small for a mat that size, or your budget is short, an 18" x 24" mat will work just fine.

Choose a mat that has a somewhat rough surface—Olfa's cutting mats are good examples of the type of surface you should look for. The slightly rough surface helps the mat grip fabric, and its self-healing properties keep the rotary blade from doing permanent damage to the mat when you cut.

Most mats have a network of square grids marked on at least one side, with ruler measurements that run along the outer edges of the grids. The grids are not accurate enough to measure the precisely cut patches you'll need for your quilts, but they are perfect for estimating dimensions and for cutting fabric pieces that needn't be exact.

Most rotary cutting mats are reversible. Some are a light, neutral color on one side and a darker color on the other. You can flip these mats over to cut on a color that contrasts with your fabric, since that makes it easier to see fabric edges. Green and gray are both commonly used colors, but manufacturers are spicing things up a bit by offering rotary cutting mats in bright shades like blue, pink, and purple.

Rotary mats are made from a rubberlike material that breaks easily when bent. Store mats flat when not in use, and prevent warping by keeping them out of direct sunlight and away from heat sources.

Rotary Cutting Safety Tips

It's important to talk about a few basic rotary cutting safety precautions before you make your first cut. I'm not trying to frighten you, but I do want you to have a healthy respect for the damage a rotary cutter can do to your body parts.

▶ Take a few minutes to read details about fabric grain in Chapter 2 before you begin to rotary cut. The information will help you understand why straight-grain strips are important for making accurate quilt components that fit together just like they should. The quick-piecing instructions in Chapter 7 are another resource that will help you understand how rotary cut strips are used.

• **Close your cutter's safety latch every time you lay it down,** even if you plan to pick it up a minute later. What if the phone rings and you step away? Or someone comes to the door? You might forget the cutter blade is exposed when you return to your sewing area and accidentally lay your hand or arm on the blade.

• **Handle replacement blades carefully.** Most blades are replaced by opening a nut and washer to remove the old blade, then reversing the process to add the new blade. Before disposing of it, place the old blade into the plastic receptacle the new blade arrived in. If you do not have a container for the blade, wrap it carefully in several layers of duct tape and place it in a solid container, such as an empty can, before putting it in the trash.

• **Always keep your new blades in a safe place—away from children and pets.** When my daughter was seven she found a new cutter and blade that I thought was tucked safely away. I doubt I've ever been more frightened than when she walked up to me with bloody hands. We were lucky because the cuts were not deep. She wouldn't go near a rotary cutter until recently—at the age of 23.

• **Use your rotary cutter for the tasks it was created for.** It isn't a handy screwdriver or a small hammer. That might sound silly, but I've seen people grab a cutter when the tool they really needed wasn't nearby. That's a great way to get hurt.

• **Always roll the cutter away from your body.** Cutting toward yourself puts your hands and the rest of your body in line with the blade. One little slip and you'll deal with a cut.

• **Keep your fingers away from the edges of the ruler.** You'll work through the steps to cut a piece of fabric in just a bit, and you'll see that your fingers must hold the ruler steady while you make a cut. Keep them away from the edges of the ruler and out of the path of the cutter.

- **Always use a rotary cutter while standing up.** It's difficult to hold a rotary cutter in the correct position when you're sitting down. If you must cut while sitting, talk to staff at your local quilt shop to learn about products that might work for you. Some quilters report that Martelli's Ergo 2000 cutter works nicely from a sitting position.

How to Rotary Cut Fabric Strips

Cutting long fabric strips across a fabric's crosswise grain is usually the first step you'll take for most rotary cutting tasks. You'll use long strips of fabric to make components for the strip-piecing technique discussed in Chapter 7, and you'll use them as a starting point when you want to cut specific patchwork shapes. It takes a little bit of practice to cut accurate strips, but there are some techniques you can use to jump-start the learning process.

Square up the leading edge of your fabric. Visit your local discount store and purchase a yard or two of inexpensive cotton practice fabric. Plain, unbleached muslin is a good choice—or check for bargains on the sale table. Use 100 percent cotton, because polyester blends tend to slip and slide around more easily under your rotary ruler. Prewash the fabric if you like, then pop it in the dryer and remove it when the cycle is complete.

Here is how to square up the leading edge of your fabric:

1. Fold the fabric along its length, selvages together. The fold should be straight, with no puckers. Getting rid of puckers usually means the selvages will not be perfectly aligned. Press lightly.

I'm left-handed. How should I arrange my fabric?

▶ Left-handed cutters should reverse the instructions, placing the square ruler near the right edge of the fabric and the long ruler to the right of it, its left edge covering the last half inch or so of fabric. Remove the square ruler and cut along the long ruler's left side.

2. Place the fabric on your rotary mat, with the fold near the bottom edge of the mat and the side to be squared on the left. The folded fabric will be about 22" tall. If your mat is smaller than that height, fold again to create four layers of fabric. Beginning quilters should stick to one fold when possible, because extra folds make errors more likely.

3. Position your square ruler with its left side near the left edge of the fabric, aligning one of its horizontal rules with the fold.

4. Place the right side of your 6" x 24" rotary ruler flush against the left side of the square ruler. Check to make sure horizontal lines on both rulers are parallel to the fold.

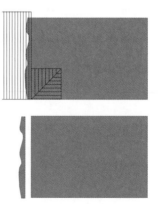

Fig. 6-1 **Align rulers and square up fabric edge**

5. Remove the square ruler. Place your left hand on the long ruler to hold it in place and roll the rotary cutter along the right edge of the ruler. Spread your fingers out to keep the ruler from slipping, but be careful to keep them out of the path of the cutter. Some quilters like to "walk" their fingers down the ruler as they cut; I usually keep my hand in one spot.

Try both to see which works best for you. The fabric's cut edge should now be at a 90-degree angle to the folded edge.

The next step is to cut strips of fabric from the squared-up edge. You'll cut long strips of fabric from the edge you just squared up. Some of the strips will be used to make quick-pieced units for your quilt blocks. Some might be used for your quilt borders, sashing, or other components. Others can be subcut to produce all sorts of different patchwork shapes.

Here is how to cut strips of fabric from the squared-up edge:

1. Practice cutting a 3" strip of fabric. Align a horizontal line on your long ruler with the bottom fold of the fabric you just squared up. Align the 3" rule line with the left edge of the fabric.
2. Hold the ruler firmly in place and roll your rotary cutter along its right edge.
3. Open the strip and inspect it. The edges of the fabric should be perfectly straight along its entire length.

Fig. 6-2 **Cutting fabric strips**

Look closely at the strip's width at the fold. If its edges at the fold are straight, like the rest of the strip, congratulations, your first two cuts were perfect. If it's bowed slightly, the leading edge was not cut at an exact 90-degree angle to the fold. Square up the fabric edge again using the two-ruler technique.

Cut another strip and check for the bend. Don't worry if your cuts aren't perfect yet—that's why you're practicing. Just keep in mind that the horizontal and vertical lines of your ruler are at a 90-degree angle to each other. If you place a horizontal line on the fold and a vertical measurement line on the cut edge your fabric will be square.

It isn't unusual for the leading edge of fabric to become out of square after several cuts, so check strips as you work to make sure they're still accurate.

It's easy to cut segments from your long strips of fabric. Before you cut segments from a strip, you'll square up its leading edge using a method that's similar to the steps you took to square up the edge of your yardage.

Here is how to square up a strip's leading edge in order to cut segments from it:

1. Place your rotary ruler near the right end of a cut strip, aligning a horizontal rule with the fabric's lower edge. Cut along the right edge of the ruler to square up the end of the strip.
2. Turn the strip around and cut segments from its left edge. Refer to the patchwork shape instructions near the end of this chapter for instructions.

Some quilters square up their yardage in the same way, by using a long ruler positioned near the right edge of the folded fabric, with a horizontal line on the fold, then cutting along the ruler's right edge. Try that method to see if it works for you. I prefer the left-edge method because to cut strips the squared-up edge must

TOOLS YOU NEED

▶ An Australian quilter designed a product called RuleSteady. Place one side of the device on your ruler and the opposite side on the rotary mat. Hold the Rule-Steady in place and cut. The ruler won't shift a bit. Read my RuleSteady review and view photos that show it in use at http://about.com/quilting/rulesteadyreview.

be flipped around to the left. I always worry that edges will shift out of place during the flip.

You can rotary cut bias strips just as easily as straight-grain strips. Long strips of fabric with their edges on the stretchy bias are used to make quilting binding. Bias strips are especially helpful when you must wrap the binding around curves that rigid straight strips can't maneuver. Bias strips are often used to make appliqué flower stems and other shapes that must be coaxed into graceful curves.

Cut long bias strips by aligning the 45-degree line on your long rotary ruler with the fold in the bottom of the fabric. Hold the ruler in place and cut along its right edge.

Now that you've experimented with rotary cutting, maybe a few more tips will help. Cutting advice sometimes makes more sense after you've actually practiced using your rotary cutting equipment. Go back and read the safety tips again, and try these tips to stay safe and perfect your rotary cutting skills.

- If you find that it's difficult to cut long, crosswise-grain strips, work with smaller pieces of fabric until you are more accustomed to rotary cutting.
- For strips with less stretch, cut along the fabric's lengthwise grain.
- Spray a little starch or sizing on prewashed fabrics to stiffen them up—they'll be easier to rotary cut.
- Attach special gripping tabs to the bottom of rotary rulers to help keep them from slipping on fabric.
- Don't stack strips to make subcuts until you've mastered rotary cutting—even if a pattern tells you to. Stacked fabric is more difficult to cut accurately.

WHAT'S HOT

▶ There are several different types of materials that can be used on the backs of your rotary rulers to help keep them in place as you cut. Adhesive backed sandpaper dots are one choice, but they do obscure rule lines where they are placed. Clear, rubber-like dots are another option. You'll also find transparent adhesive sheets with a rough surface that can be stuck to the entire reverse side of rulers.

- Change your rotary blade if fabric is more difficult to cut easily or if the blade is leaving uncut areas along your fabric.
- Be careful not to roll your cutter over straight pins or other objects. You might damage the blade or the object it touches.

How to Cut Patchwork Shapes

Now that you can cut fabric strips it's time to move on to patchwork shapes. And you know what that means—no more templates! You'll see how easy it is to use the lines on your rotary ruler to cut all sorts of shapes from a long strip of fabric. Grab your practice muslin and get ready to learn how to cut squares, rectangles, triangles, diamonds, and more.

Get started by learning how to cut squares, rectangles, and bars. All three of these shapes are cut using the horizontal and vertical lines on your rotary ruler. Squares have four 90-degree angles, also called right angles, and four equal sides. Rectangles have four right angles and are exactly twice as long as they are wide. Bars are simply long rectangles. All three shapes are found as is in quilts, but they are also a starting point for cutting other patchwork shapes.

Here is how to cut squares, rectangles, and bars using your rotary ruler:

1. Rotary cut a long strip of fabric that is ½" wider than the height of the finished square, rectangle, or bar. The additional fabric compensates for the ¼" seam allowances that will eventually be sewn along two sides of the shape.
2. Use your rotary cutting equipment to square up one end of the fabric strip.
3. Use your rotary ruler to cut away segments that are ½" longer than the finished patch length in order to compensate

for seam allowances on two more sides. Remember to keep right angles accurate by aligning a horizontal ruler line along the bottom of the fabric and placing the vertical measuring line along the leading edge.

Fig. 6-3 **Cutting squares and rectangles**

Move on to triangles next. Triangles have three sides and three angles, so at least one edge of a triangle is cut along the fabric's stretchy bias. Handle triangles with care to keep their shapes intact. Some of the triangles you'll use in quilts can be assembled using piecing techniques that let you avoid handling individual patches, but there are many times when single shapes are required.

We'll start with half-square triangles, one of the most commonly used quilting shapes. The name describes this triangle perfectly—it's the shape you get by splitting a square in half diagonally from one corner to another.

Here is how to cut half-square triangles:

1. Cut a strip of fabric that's ⅞" wider than the finished length of a half-square triangle's short sides.
2. Cut a square from the fabric by measuring and slicing a segment that is as wide as the strip is tall.
3. Cut each square in half once diagonally to produce two half-square triangles. Repeat to make more triangles. The long edge of the triangle is cut on the bias.

Fig. 6-4 **Cutting half-square triangles**

Quarter-square triangles look exactly like half-square triangles, but they are actually very different. The fabric's straight grain runs with the long edge of a quarter-square triangle. Quarter-square triangles are used to fill in the jagged edges of a quilt with blocks set on point. Their long, straight-grain edges help keep the quilt's perimeter from stretching during final assembly. The triangles are also used in many other ways.

Here is how to cut quarter-square triangles:

1. Cut a fabric strip that is 1¼" wider than the finished length of the triangle's longest edge.
2. Cut square segments from the strip using the same measurement.
3. Cut each square in half twice diagonally to make four quarter-square triangles. Cut additional squares and triangles as needed.

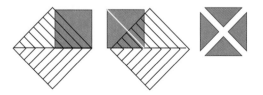

Fig. 6-5 **Cutting quarter-square triangles**

Scalene triangles have three unequal sides. The scalene triangle quilters use most often is the right scalene triangle, also called a long triangle. You can easily cut long triangles from rectangles.

Here is how to cut scalene triangles:

1. Cut a strip of fabric that is $^{11}/_{16}$" wider than the finished length of the long triangle's shortest side. Most rotary cutters are not marked in sixteenth-inch increments, so you'll need to estimate.
2. Cut a rectangle from the strip that is $^{5}/_{16}$" longer than the finished length of the long triangle.
3. Cut the rectangle in half once diagonally to make two long triangles.

Sometimes you'll need to cut long triangles that are mirror images of each other. To make mirror images of the first triangles, cut another rectangle diagonally but from opposite corners, as shown in the inset in the Figure 6-6, cutting long triangles.

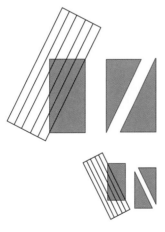

Fig. 6-6 **Cutting long triangles**

You can rotary cut long triangles from bars, but their seam allowances vary depending on triangle lengths. Use a piece of graph paper to discover dimensions, then cut with your rotary equipment.

Here is how to cut long triangles:

1. Draw a finished size long triangle on graph paper and add a ¼" seam allowance to each side. Measure the triangle's length and height, including seam allowances.
2. Cut strips of fabric that match the triangle's height. Cut bars from the strip to match its length.
3. Divide each bar once diagonally to produce long triangles. Cut mirror image triangles if necessary.

Equilateral triangles measure the same length on each of their three sides, with 60-degree angles at all corners. You'll see them used in many ways. Equilateral triangles are the only shape used in the traditional Thousand Pyramids quilt.

Here is how to cut equilateral triangles:

1. Measure the distance from the midpoint of an equilateral triangle's base to the tip of the point just above it. Use the desired finished size of the triangle.
2. Add ¾" to the measurement and cut a strip of fabric that width.
3. Align the 60-degree line of a rotary ruler with the long edge of the fabric strip as shown in Figure 6-7.
4. Make a cut along the right edge of the ruler. Discard the piece you cut off or put it in your scrap bag.

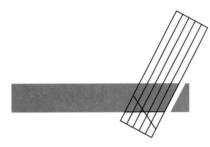

Fig. 6-7 **Prepare the strip edge**

5. Rotate the ruler, aligning its other 60-degree line along the bottom edge of the fabric strip. Position the edge of the ruler so that it forms a point at the bottom edge of the first cut.
6. Cut along the right side of the ruler to create an equilateral triangle. All three legs should be the same length and that length should be ⅞" longer than the triangle's finished size.

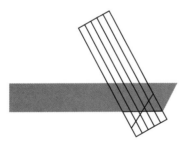

Fig. 6-8 **Cutting the first equilateral triangle**

Now it's time to learn how to cut diamonds. A diamond is a square that's been flattened a bit. It has four sides of equal length, just like the original square, but its corners are no longer 90-degree angles. Quilting patterns generally use diamonds with either 30-degree, 45-degree, or 60-degree angles at their narrow points. All three types of diamonds are cut from strips of fabric that are ½" taller than the finished height of the diamond.

Here is how to cut diamonds:

1. Cut a strip of fabric that's ½" wider than the diamond's finished height.
2. Align the ruler's 30-degree, 45-degree, or 60-degree line with the left lower edge of the fabric. Slide the ruler far enough on to the strip so that there's fabric under its entire right edge.
3. Cut along the right edge of the ruler to create the first angled side.

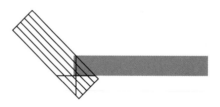

Fig. 6-9 **Preparing the fabric edge**

4. Find the line on the rotary ruler that matches the height of the fabric strip. Match that line with the angled left edge of the fabric and align the degree line with the bottom edge of the strip.
5. Cut along the right side of the ruler to create the diamond.

ELSEWHERE ON THE WEB

▶ Jinny Beyer offers lots of free patterns on her Web site. One is a beginner's pattern for the Thousand Pyramids quilt, which is made from equilateral triangles. You'll love the color play in this quilt—it proves that one-shape quilts can be every bit as interesting as quilts made from intricately pieced blocks. Search for *thousand pyramids* on the site http:// jinnybeyer.com.

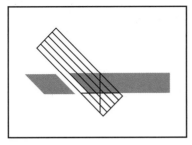
Fig. 6-10 **Cutting the first diamond**

Practice cutting different patchwork shapes until you feel comfortable with the steps required for each one. It won't take long for you to remember which seam allowances to add and how to align the ruler for each different patchwork shape.

Get Linked

There are many rotary cutting resources online. You'll find a library of ideas on my Quilting Web site at About.com.

HOW TO CHOOSE A ROTARY CUTTER

Additional details about rotary cutters, with photos to show you how they differ.

http://about.com/quilting/rotaryskills

QUILTING TOOL REVIEWS

Keep up to date by reading reviews for a variety of tools made just for quilters.

http://about.com/quilting/equipmentreviews

FREE QUILT PATTERNS

Most of the quilt patterns on my Web site are assembled using rotary cutting techniques. You'll find patterns for every skill level, beginner to advanced.

http://about.com/quilting/freepatterns

Chapter 7

Piecing Your Quilts

Machine Piecing Basics

The act of sewing together patches to make a quilt is called piecing. It can be done by machine or by hand. The two techniques are very different, and most quilters tend to choose one or the other to make most of their quilts but sometimes will switch back and forth between techniques depending on what they want to achieve.

Machine piecing lets you see results in a hurry, and sometimes that's the best motivation for finishing one project and starting another. Hand piecing is perfect for quiet times, such as when you're watching television with the family or when you would like a portable project to take with you on a trip. I nearly always took handwork along to keep me occupied during waiting room stays at my daughter's dancing and music lessons.

The majority of today's quilters use a sewing machine to assemble their quilts, even if they finish them with hand quilting. You don't hear too many people arguing anymore that it's more traditional to

About®

sew a quilt by hand than by machine. Past generations of quilters sewed everything by hand because they often had no other choice! I'm willing to bet that the majority of them would work on one of our modern sewing machines in a heartbeat. Machine piecing makes it possible to finish a quilt in a much shorter time, and a quick finish is a reward that motivates you to start another project.

Sewing a Quarter-Inch Seam

Nearly all of the quilt components you'll sew will have a quarter-inch seam allowance. If you're new to sewing it won't be difficult to become accustomed to that width. If you've sewn lots of clothing, which is typically made with much wider seam allowances, it might take you a little longer to feel comfortable with the reduction. Follow these instructions, practice a bit, and it won't be long until your quarter-inch seams are perfect every time.

You'll need your normal sewing gear to set up a quarter-inch seam allowance. That includes a rotary cutter, mat, 24" ruler, an iron and ironing board, and a sewing machine. If you have a quarter-inch presser foot, put it on the machine. Otherwise, use your standard presser foot and find a roll of masking tape. You'll also need several scraps of dark and light fabrics that measure at least 2" x 4".

Let's check your seam allowance first, to see if it's already accurate. Cut two 2" x 4" light fabric strips and a dark strip of the same size.

Then, to continue checking your seam allowance:

1. Align a 2" x 4" light fabric strip with a dark strip, placing right sides together. Make sure edges all match.
2. Sew the patches together lengthwise, feeding them through the machine and aligning their right edges to sew what you think is a ¼" seam allowance. If you have a quarter-inch presser foot, the right edges of the stacked fabrics should be

aligned with the right edge of the presser foot as they move through the machine.

3. Sew another light fabric strip to the opposite edge of the dark strip.

4. Remove the unit from your sewing machine. Carefully press seam allowances toward the dark strip. Refer to the pressing instructions later in this chapter if you're not sure how to press seam allowances.

5. Use a rotary ruler to measure the dark center strip. It should be exactly 1½" wide along its entire length. Each of the two outer strips should measure exactly 1¾" wide along their entire lengths.

If strip dimensions are accurate—congratulations! You're ready to assemble a quilt. If strip dimension aren't quite what they should be, it's time to make a few changes that will help you sew accurate quarter-inch seams.

Let's inspect the unit carefully before you change your sewing style. Strip dimensions can be off for several reasons—it might not be your seam allowance at all. Don't change your sewing setup until you've considered a few other common problems.

- Did you press seam allowances thoroughly? If not, your unit might have a little extra width tied up in the slight height, or loft, created on the front of patches when seam allowances are sewn to one side. Press the seam allowances again and check strip width.

- Make sure that fabric edges didn't move away from each other when you sewed the seam. If edges are not aligned the finished patches will not be accurate. Next time, secure

WHAT'S HOT

▶ Some quilters use straight pins to secure every seam they sew. I don't always use pins to secure short patches unless the fabrics I'm using seem to slip around under the presser foot. Try it both ways to see which works best for you. When you use straight pins, remove them as the needle approaches to prevent broken needles. Use long, thin straight pins with large heads that are easy to see on your patchwork.

with straight pins or place a warm iron onto aligned patches before you sew them. Heat helps fabric pieces stick to each other.

- If seams are irregular—wide in some places and narrow in others—you may be sewing too fast. It's easier to sew accurately when you don't try to rush through a seam. Set your machine to sew on a reduced speed, if possible, or lighten up on the foot pedal.
- Try changing your needle position. Move the needle a notch to the right if your seam allowance is too large (strips are too narrow). Move it a notch to the left if the seam allowance is too short (strips are too wide).
- If you're using a quarter-inch presser foot, guide the fabric under it at a slightly different position.

Cut and sew a second set of strips to correct any of those assembly problems, then press and measure. If the unit still isn't accurate, don't worry, because we can change the way you sew a quarter-inch seam. Cut a few more sets of 2" x 4" dark and light strips to use in your tests.

Add a guide to your sewing machine's throat plate. Most sewing machines have a series of vertical lines etched into their throat plates—the little metal piece that surrounds the area where the needle moves up and down. Place a clear rotary ruler under the needle and bring the needle gently down by hand until it just barely touches a line on the ruler. Look to the right. Is there an etched line that's ¼" from the line the needle is resting on? That's your quarter-inch seam guide.

The etched line will help guide you to sew a quarter-inch seam, but you might discover that it's not 100 percent accurate, or that it's difficult to keep fabric edges aligned with it as you sew. Your machine might not even have a quarter-inch line on its throat plate. It's easy to fix the problem.

Here is how to add a guide to your sewing machine's throat plate:

1. Place a rotary ruler under the sewing machine needle, its first ¼" line just below the needle's tip.
2. Check to make sure the ruler is straight. Nearby grooves in the throat plate should be parallel with the ruler's edge.
3. Place a 1" piece of masking tape on the throat plate with its left edge aligned against the right edge of the ruler. Remove the ruler.
4. Sew another test unit. Guide the right edge of your fabric along the left edge of the masking tape. Press the unit and measure the width of its strips.
5. If the unit is accurate, your seam allowance is correct. Stack additional pieces of masking tape on top of the first to build up a ridge for fabrics to butt against. You can achieve height quickly by rotary cutting a piece of adhesive backed mole-skin, sold at your local pharmacy, and applying it on top of the tape.
6. If seam allowances are still off, move the tape and try again. Continue moving the tape and testing units until you are sewing a quarter-inch seam.

Accurate seams are nearly always what we call scant quarter-inch seams. A scant quarter-inch seam is a seam that's a hair's length shorter than ¼". That's usually the width that turns out to be ideal, and it has a lot to do with our rotary cutting techniques.

Rotary-cut pieces are usually very slightly smaller than patches cut with templates because the lines we used to mark around shapes are missing. Pencil lines aren't very wide, but most of us

TOOLS YOU NEED

▶ Sewing machine makers cater to quilters because they know we'll buy the tools we need to make our quilts. Most new machines either come with a quarter-inch presser foot or have one that's available as an option. Bernina has two, a standard patchwork foot that helps you sew ¼" or ⅛" seams, and a second foot with a guide on its right edge to butt fabric against. Quilting accessory companies make quarter-inch feet to fit nearly all sewing machines.

tend to cut on the outside of them, adding just a tiny bit of width to our patches. The width we gained was just enough to compensate for the loft that gets lost in a quarter-inch seam when it's pressed to one side.

Rotary-cut patches are missing that little extra line, and sewing a scant seam usually compensates for the problem. Accuracy takes practice, but keep at it and it won't be too long before you know exactly where to position your ruler when you cut and exactly how to feed units through the machine to achieve the best results.

Sewing Patches and Blocks Together

When you machine piece, you'll always sew from one end of the matched patches to the other unless you are setting in a seam or the pattern tells you to sew partial seams for another reason. For most quilt blocks, fabric patches are aligned with their right sides together for sewing.

When adjacent patches have edges of the same length, like a square sewn to a square or a triangle sewn to another identical triangle, their edges match exactly and are easy to align. When patches of adjacent shapes are different it can be a little trickier to determine how they should fit together.

The most common unmatched scenario is a square or rectangle that's sewn to the long edge of a triangle. The angled tips of the triangle always extend past the edge of the other shape's 90-degree corners, making it more difficult to align patches for sewing. Try folding each patch in half to find its midpoint along the side to be sewn, and then match the midpoints when you align the pieces. An alternative is to measure ¼" inward from each side of both patches. Seams end where seam allowances intersect. Match the pieces and place the patches right sides together and pin-match

▶ Be sure to change your sewing machine needle before each new project. Needles are inexpensive, so it's definitely not worth it to let a dull or damaged needle spoil even one seam in your quilts. A universal needle will work fine for piecing your quilts.

the seam endings. Remember that seam lines match even if seam allowances do not. If the endpoints of adjacent seams match each other your patches will fit together perfectly.

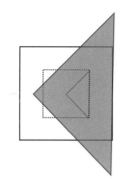

Fig. 7-1 Match seam lines to align patches

Quilt blocks are assembled piece by piece, then row by row. Individual quilt pieces are usually sewn together to make rows for a quilt block, then rows are sewn together to complete the block. Most seams are sewn all the way across the rows, just as they are when assembling individual patches.

Remember the loft issue I talked about earlier—where the fabric in a seam allowance makes the fabric above it puff out just a bit? That characteristic provides a handy tool when it's time to sew pieces and rows together. By pressing seams in adjoining rows in opposite directions the opposing lofts butt into each other to create a snug fit when we align patches right sides together for sewing—and that helps you match seams perfectly.

Fig. 7-2 Using loft to match seams

New quilters usually start sewing by following a printed quilting pattern, and nearly all patterns tell you which way to press seams. Pay special attention to pressing directions and watch how perfectly your units fit together, then use the technique whenever you design a quilt or block of your own. You'll see firsthand how loft works when you make practice pieces later in the chapter.

Learn how to sew a set-in seam. Some quilt blocks can't be assembled by sewing components together with continuous seams. We use a technique called setting in when pieces must be inserted into an opening around previously joined patches. The most important thing to remember about set-in quilt pieces is that your seam should never extend into seam allowances.

The corners of mitered quilt borders are assembled using the setting-in technique. You'll find those instructions in Chapter 4. The technique can be adapted for any patch that uses set-in seams.

How to Press Your Quilt Components

Thoroughly pressing your components and their seam allowances helps eliminate those little widths of fabric that get tied up in loft. Leaving too much loft tied up in seams creates distortions in your patches, and components that aren't the right size won't match up correctly when it's time to sew them together. Pressing after each step might seem like a bother and a waste of time, but you'll love the time you save when all of your quilting units fit together just like they should—without ripping out seams and tugging and pulling to make them match.

Notice that quilters call this technique pressing, not ironing. Remembering the differences between those two terms will help you from the very first time you turn on the iron. Press the iron onto your quilt blocks and other components, letting the heat and the weight of the iron do the work. Never iron vigorously back and forth—that's one of the best ways I know to stretch your quilt out of shape. There are times you'll need to move the iron a bit. Just take a bit of care and move the iron carefully across the fabric.

Follow these steps to press a quilting unit. You'll start pressing pieced units as you make them so that they're ready to sew to their neighbors when it's time to assemble a block. Use these general instructions to start practicing.

1. Make a handy practice unit by sewing together two of the short strips leftover from testing your seam allowance earlier in this chapter.
2. Turn your iron to the cotton setting. Place the sewn strip unit on your ironing board unopened, just as it was sewn. The seam allowance will be pressed toward the fabric that is on top.
3. Place the iron straight down on the unopened unit to set the seam.
4. Let the unit cool a little and then flip the top fabric back gently, using your fingertips to open it along the seam line.
5. Place the edge of the iron on the lower strip and gently work it toward and over the seam allowance. Take care, too much of a push and you could stretch the fabric.
6. Bring the iron up and then place it flat on the unit again, allowing its weight to finish pressing the seam flat.
7. Turn the unit over and press from the back to complete the job.

Most quilters press seam allowances to one side instead of open. Some feel that it strengthens seams to do that, but I press to the side because of the match factor we talked about in the Piecing section. There are situations where pressing seams open

ASK YOUR GUIDE

▶ *Should I press my quilt blocks with steam or use a dry iron?*

That's a good question, and quilters have different opinions about the answer. I don't use steam because fabrics stretch more easily when they are hot and damp. I do keep a spray bottle filled with water on my ironing board because sometimes I need to square up a skewed block— in that case the stretch is welcome! The spray lets me put moisture exactly where I want it. Try both steam and dry settings to see which works best for you.

will help the block lay flatter—such as when you're assembling units with lots of seams that come together in one spot. Don't be afraid to press seams open if it helps you make a more accurate quilt block.

Learn Quick-Piecing Techniques

Quick-piecing techniques allow us to sew large pieces of fabric together in specific configurations, then cut identical segments away from the large units. The segments can represent entire rows of a quilt block or just one multi-unit piece. Quick piecing allows you to make quilting components without working with small pieces of fabric—a significant time savings.

Strip piecing is one form of quick piecing. You learned to cut long strips of fabric in Chapter 6, and then you learned to cut individual patches from them. Strip piecing is a way to use those long strips to make multipiece units without handling individual pieces of fabric. The majority of quilt patterns you'll find in new books and magazines are assembled using strip-piecing techniques, so it's an important method to get comfortable with.

First we'll assemble units called **strip sets** by sewing together long pieces of fabric in different configurations. Then we'll cut segments from the sets and sew them back together in different ways. Let's practice by making a 12" double nine-patch block. The strip lengths are slightly longer than necessary to allow for squaring up edges as you cut segments from them.

Use scraps if you like—they don't have to match. Or follow a color scheme that matches your décor and use the finished 18" block to make a throw pillow cover. You'll find instructions to do that near the end of Chapter 14.

Fig. 7-3 Double nine-patch block layout

CUTTING CHART FOR DOUBLE NINE-PATCH BLOCK

Fabric	Patch Size	Number Required
Dark	2½" x 27"	2
Dark	2½" x 14"	1
Light	2½" x 27"	1
Light	2½" x 14"	2
Light	6½" x 6½"	4

Here is how to practice strip piecing by making a 12" double nine-patch block:

1. Sew a 2½" x 27" dark strip lengthwise to one side of the 2½" x 27" light strip. Repeat to sew a second dark strip of the same length to the opposite side of the light strip.
2. Press both seam allowances toward the dark side strips.
3. Using the rotary cutting instructions in Chapter 6 as a guide, square up one end of the strip set. Cut ten 2½" wide segments from the squared up edge. Set aside.

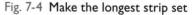

Fig. 7-4 **Make the longest strip set**

4. Sew a 2½" × 14" light strip lengthwise to one side of the 2½" × 14" dark strip. Repeat to sew a second light strip of the same length to the opposite side of the light strip.
5. Press the seam allowances toward the dark center strip.
6. Square up one end of the strip set. Cut five 2½" wide segments from the squared up edge.

Fig. 7-5 **Make the short strip set**

7. Arrange two of the segments cut in step 3 with one segment from step 6. Make three rows, placing the segment with a dark center strip in the middle.
8. Sew the rows together, butting seam allowances to achieve a perfect match at intersections. Repeat to make a total of five identical nine-patch units.

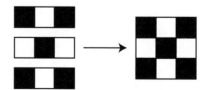

Fig. 7-6 **Make a small nine-patch unit**

9. Refer back to the double nine-patch block layout in Figure 7-3. Arrange the five small nine-patch units into three rows, placing the light 6½" × 6½" plain squares next to them as shown. The nine-patch units create an X shape within the block when the rows are arranged correctly.
10. Sew the three units in each row together, pressing seam allowances toward the large squares.
11. Sew the rows together, butting seam allowances for a perfect match at seam intersections.

You can use strip-piecing techniques to make thousands of quilt blocks. Practice the method by making the Shades of the Past quilt in Chapter 15. You'll find a link to additional strip-pieced patterns at the end of this chapter.

It's easy to make quick-pieced, half-square triangle units. One of the most useful quick-piecing techniques you'll find is a method that helps you sew half-square triangle units together without manipulating their stretchy bias edges. These units are one of the most versatile components in a quilt, so you'll see them used often in blocks and borders. There are many ways to quick piece them, but this method is my favorite. Use squares with sides that are ⅞" longer than the finished size of the half-square triangles. Use a light and a dark 3⅞" square for this practice session.

Here is how to practice quick piecing half-square triangle units:

1. Use a pencil or permanent marker to draw a diagonal line from one corner to the opposite corner on the reverse side of the light square. Draw a line ¼" from each side of the first if you do not have a quarter-inch presser foot.

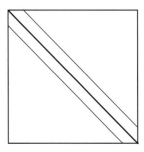

Fig. 7-7 Make a quick-pieced, half-square triangle unit

▶ I often cut my squares a little larger than the required size, then align finished units under a rotary ruler and trim them back to the exact size the pattern calls for. That technique is especially helpful when making miniature quilts, since tiny differences impact little blocks. Martingale's Bias Square ruler is a good choice for this method. It has a diagonal line and markings on sides that help you make sure each half of the unit is exactly the same.

2. Place the light square against the dark square, right sides together and all edges aligned.
3. Sew two seams, each one ¼" from the marked center line, using your presser foot or premarked lines as a guide.
4. Use scissors or rotary cutting equipment to cut through both layers of the square on the unsewn center line.
5. Place the two resulting units on the ironing board, darkest triangle up. Press flat to set the seam.
6. Open up one unit and use your fingers to press the fabric back along the seam line. Press.
7. Trim off the triangular nubs that extend past the corners along the seam line.
8. Repeat to press the second unit.

Measure the units. They should measure 3½" square. If they are smaller, press again and measure. If they are still too small, make another set and use a scant quarter-inch seam allowance. Units are rarely larger than they should be.

Use chain piecing to speed up your sewing tasks. Think of chain piecing as assembly-line sewing. When you're ready to sew, align your units and stack them near your sewing machine. Sew units together, feeding them under the presser foot in a continuous chain without breaking threads between pairs. Remove the chained pieces from the machine when all are sewn together and cut the threads between them. Press and move on to the next task.

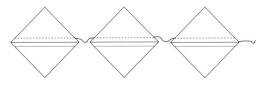

Fig. 7-8 Chain piecing the half-square triangle units

Hand Sewing Quilt Blocks

Some quilters love to hand piece, and it's the only way they even consider making a quilt. Hand sewing gives them a personal bond with their work, and sitting down with a needle and thread is very often their way of relaxing. You'll find that hand piecing gives you lots of control over the patches in your quilt blocks. Another plus, there's no need to get up and press every time you add a patch.

Every quilter should learn a few hand-piecing basics. Even if it's not a method you want to use often, you'll find that it will help you assemble some types of units that can't be dealt with as accurately on the machine.

Traditional hand piecers use templates to cut patches.
I haven't talked much about templates in this book, because most patches used in it are rotary cut. This chapter is probably the perfect place to talk a bit about them. Templates are exact copies of a pattern. Piecing templates usually include a seam allowance around all sides of the shape.

Generations of quilters have made templates from any type of stiff material they could find. Cardboard was a traditional favorite

ASK YOUR GUIDE

What's your favorite type of iron?

▶ The brand of iron you purchase doesn't really matter, but look for one that's heavy. Quilters press instead of ironing back and forth, so a combination of heat and weight makes it easy to remove wrinkles and press nice, crisp seams.

▸ It's important to know where all seam intersections are in a hand-pieced block, because that's where you always stop sewing. Hand piecers make traditional templates with seam allowances, and then mark inward to define seam lines. Next they use a ¹⁄₁₆" paper punch to remove a tiny circle at each seam intersection. When they mark the shape's cutting line, they can mark through the hole at the same time to define seam ends. Fiskars sells a nice ¹⁄₁₆" hole punch at www.fiskarscrafts.com/tools/t_hand-punch-116-circle.aspx.

for creating rigid templates that were durable enough to stay in shape as a marking pencil was used to trace around them. Today you'll find numerous commercially made template materials, including gridded and plain transparent plastic.

Window templates are a good choice for hand piecers. They are made by tracing two sets of lines onto the template material—the outer cutting line and the inner seam line. Marked seam lines are important when you hand piece because, unlike machine piecing, you never sew into the seam allowance when assembling a quilt block by hand.

Fig. 7-9 **Example of a window template**

Place the template right-side down on the reverse side of fabric and mark around the outside edge and the inside opening. Cut out the fabric on the outer lines. You'll use the inner lines later to help you sew accurate seams.

If you want to speed things up, rotary cut your patches. Place the window template right-side down on the reverse of each patch, aligning its outer edges with the edges of the fabric. Hold the template in place and mark around the inner window to define seam lines.

Learn a few hand-piecing basics. This book focuses on machine sewing, but let's try a few hand-piecing basics to help you become familiar with the method. Cut two half-square triangles of any matching size and mark the seam lines on the reverse of each one, stopping when you reach the seam allowances. Align the triangles right sides together, marking seam ends with pins. Use extra pins to secure the edges.

Thread a thin sewing needle with about 20" of cotton thread that's knotted at one end. Remove a pin that marks one end of the seam on your matched triangles. Insert the sewing needle into the same hole. Use a small running stitch—straight stitches—to sew along the entire length of the seam, taking a backstitch about every ¾" or so to add stability. Check the opposite side of the pair occasionally to make sure your seam line is staying on its marked line. When you reach the end of the seam, stop sewing and backstitch.

Make another identical unit. Place the two units right sides together—it doesn't matter which sides are aligned for this simple practice. Sew the units together using the same technique you used to attach individual patches. Sew only through seam lines, not into the seam allowance. All hand-sewn patches are assembled in the same way. Press the unit when it's finished.

WHAT'S HOT

▶ The hand-piecing instructions here are very brief and only intended to give you a few basics about the technique. We have a very active group of talented hand piecers on our Quilting Forum—all members who love to help newcomers learn the art of hand piecing. If it's a technique you are interested in I encourage you to stop by the Quilting Forum (look for the Hand Piecing folder), read the messages, and get involved in their ongoing projects. Visit http://about .com/quilting/forum.

Get Linked

There are many more ways to use quick-piecing techniques. My Quilting Web site on About.com includes tutorials to help you master a variety of quick-piecing methods.

QUARTER-SQUARE TRIANGLE UNITS

Another popular quick-pieced unit is the quarter-square triangle unit, where four equally sized triangles occupy quadrants of a square. You'll find illustrations and assembly instructions on my Web site.

↗ http://about.com/quilting/quartersquaretriangles

MAKE HALF-SQUARE TRIANGLES ON A LONG GRID

There are other quick ways to make half-square triangle units. One easy method lets you assemble them by sewing together two long strips of fabric. The instructions on this page explain how to use that easy technique.

↗ http://about.com/quilting/halfsquaretriangles

Chapter 8

Learn to Foundation Piece

Introduction to Foundation Piecing

Foundation piecing is a broad term that actually describes several different patchwork techniques. The commonly used term for one popular method is paper piecing, but even that phrase has different meanings. You'll discover one thing as you sort through the foundation piecing instructions in this chapter—it's an easy technique. Once you've made a few quilt blocks you'll instinctively know how to assemble any foundation-pieced project. When you foundation piece you'll sew pieces of fabric directly onto a template—the foundation. Some **foundation templates** are an exact replica of an entire block or portion of a block, complete with seam lines. Other types, like the string-pieced table runner in Chapter 11, are designed for freehand sewing.

You can use temporary foundations to construct your quilt blocks. Temporary foundations are removed after quilt blocks are joined but before the quilt is sandwiched with batting and backing.

About.

Paper is probably the most widely used temporary foundation, but there are several products that have been developed especially for foundation piecing. Some are torn away after the block is assembled and some dissolve the first time you wash the quilt.

Temporary foundations are removed, so they don't stick around to make your quilts bulky, which makes it much easier to hand quilt the project. However, it can be time consuming to remove temporary foundations, especially from miniature quilt blocks with lots of tiny patches. One trick that makes the job easier is to use a shorter than normal stitch length when you sew onto temporary foundations. The short stitches help perforate the foundation along seam lines, making it easier to remove later. Shorter stitches also help keep seams intact when you tear away the foundation. There is a drawback to short stitches—they can be difficult to rip out if you make an error.

You can use any type of lightweight copier paper for foundations, especially if you plan to print the patterns with a copy machine or printer connected to your computer. Smooth vellum works well and so does blank newsprint, but both are tricky to use in printers—you'll probably need to mark patterns onto them in other ways.

Some quilters prefer to use permanent foundations. Permanent foundations remain in the quilt forever. Muslin is a traditional permanent foundation, but you can also sew onto nonwoven interfacing or any other sheer material. Fabric foundations tend to stretch a bit as you handle them, so stiffen them up before you sew by spritzing on a little spray starch. Using a dry iron during block assembly also helps you avoid stretch.

Like temporary foundations, permanent foundations come with their own set of pros and cons. They remain in the block to stabilize patches, so you can use up bits and pieces of your fabric stash without too much regard to where stretchy bias edges will be placed.

Because you won't tug along seams to remove them, blocks with permanent foundations can be sewn with longer stitches, making mistakes easier to correct. There's another plus: Many blocks made with permanent foundations don't need to be quilted heavily. The foundation itself adds a bit of depth to your piece.

On the down side, hand quilting is usually not possible when you use permanent foundations, so plan to machine quilt or tie those projects. A permanent foundation remains in the seam allowances when blocks are joined together, where it sometimes creates quite a bit of bulk, making it difficult to press seams neatly.

Foundation Piece a Small Quilt Block

The best way to learn how to foundation piece is to make a quilt block. We'll make a foundation template from paper and sew directly on it to create Courthouse Steps, a variation of the Log Cabin block. This is the technique most people are referring to when they say "paper piecing." It's nothing like English paper piecing, which is covered later in the chapter. Quilters also call this method flip and sew and sew and flip. All of those terms became popularly used names for the technique because they describe how fabric is manipulated when we sew it to the foundation.

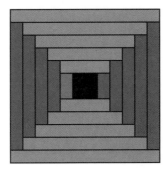

Fig. 8-1 Courthouse Steps block

ELSEWHERE ON THE WEB

▶ Carol Doak has developed her own brand of foundation paper. It feeds evenly through copiers and inkjet and laser printers, and it tears away more easily than typical bond paper does. Carol's paper is sheer, so it doesn't add a lot of bulk in the seams when you join adjacent patches. You can order the paper and other helpful foundation-piecing supplies directly from Carol at www.caroldoak .com/store.php.

▸ We have a photo gallery on the About.com Quilting site that's devoted to Log Cabin, Pineapple, and other similar foundation-pieced quilts. The projects in the gallery are an excellent illustration of the different layouts you'll find for one simple pattern. If you're into vibrant colors and well done color value placement, be sure to take a look at this gallery at http://about.com/quilting/logcabin.

Flip to the Courthouse Steps template in Appendix C. Scan the template into your computer at 200 percent. The pattern should now measure 6" square. I did not include a seam allowance around the pattern because it would have been distorted when you enlarged it. Use a ruler to draw lines around the template, ¼" from each side. The lines represent the seam allowance you'll need when blocks are sewn together side by side. They are the only visible seam allowances in the block.

Insert a new universal sewing needle in your sewing machine. The needle will get a good workout as it travels through paper and fabric. You'll need a sharp pair of scissors to trim seam allowances as you work on the block. Rotary cutting equipment is helpful for cutting strips of fabric, and a few straight pins will come in handy.

To make the block you'll need a piece of red fabric that measures about 2" square. You'll also need eight different dark fabrics and eight different light fabrics. Cut strips from each, making them about 1¾" wide. Length depends on their position in the block, but no strip needs to be more than 8" long. If you don't have a large collection of fabrics it's fine to use a smaller variety and repeat fabrics within the block.

You might wonder why I stipulated a red square in the instructions. It's used in the center of the block, a spot that's traditionally red to signify the heart or hearth of a log cabin. Choose another color if you prefer.

For this technique, all seams are sewn on the front or marked side of the foundation template. All fabric is positioned on the reverse or unmarked side.

Here is how to foundation piece once you have enlarged the Courthouse Steps template:

1. Cut out the template to make it easier to handle, but leave an inch or so of paper past the outer seam line. Place the red square right-side up on the unprinted side of the template, centering it within the square marked "1" on the pattern—printed lines are usually visible through the paper. Secure the fabric with a straight pin. The first piece is the only fabric that will be positioned right-side up.

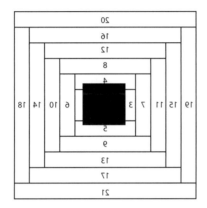

Fig. 8-2 **Center the square patch on the unprinted side of the template**

2. Turn the template over to the printed side and hold it up to the light. Inspect the shadow of the red square. Its edges should overlap the boundaries of piece 1 by ¼" or so. It needn't be perfectly centered, but the overlaps will become your seam allowance. If any side has a skimpy allowance—less than ³⁄₁₆"—reposition and check again.

3. Select a dark fabric strip for piece 2. Leave the strip long and cut it back after sewing or trim it now to the approximate length of the center square. Lay the strip right-side down on top of the square, aligning its left edge with the side of the square adjacent to the patch labeled "2."

Which type of foundation do you prefer, permanent or temporary?

▶ I like to use temporary foundations most of the time, even though I sometimes get impatient when it's time to remove them. I don't like the bulky seams of permanent foundations, and I feel like fabric templates always stretch out of shape at least a little bit during assembly.

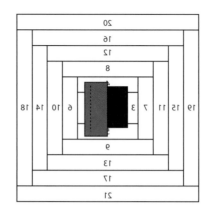

Fig. 8-3 **Sew piece 2 to the template**

▶ Foundation piecing is an excellent method to use when you want to construct dollhouse miniature quilts. It does take a little while to assemble the tiny quilts, but they can be every bit as intricate as regular quilts—and no one will guess how easy they were to make. Chapter 10 includes information about dollhouse quilts, and you'll find dollhouse quilt patterns on the About.com Quilting Web site at http://about.com/quilting/dollhouse quilts.

4. Hold the fabrics in place and turn the foundation over. Sew a seam on the line that separates the center patch 1 with patch 2. Begin and end the seam a few stitches on either side of the line. Remove the block from the sewing machine.

5. Trim the excess tail of dark fabric if necessary and flip piece 2 right-side up. Hold it up to the light, printed side facing you. The shadow of piece 2 should overlap the lines that surround its perimeter by enough to create a stable seam when you sew on those lines.

6. If the piece is correct, trim up the seam allowance if necessary to reduce bulk. Press or finger press the patch in place.

7. Add piece 3 in the same way, but position it right-side down along the opposite site of the center square. Hold fabrics in place and flip the foundation right-side up. Sew on the line that separates piece 1 from piece 3, starting and stopping a few stitches on either side of the line.

8. Finger press piece 3 right-side up and check its position as you did for other patches. Trim the seam allowance to reduce bulk if necessary and press the patch in place.

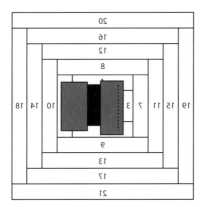

Fig. 8-4 **Sew piece 3 to the template**

9. Choose a light fabric for piece 4. Trim its length to match the length across patches 1, 2, and 3 or use it long and trim back after sewing. Place the strip right-side down, aligning its edge along the combined width of pieces 1 to 3. Hold the strip in place and turn the foundation over. Sew on the line separating the bottom edges of the first three pieces, beginning and ending a few stitches on either side of the line.

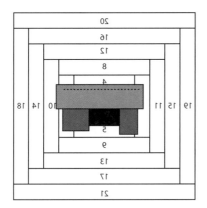

Fig. 8-5 **Sew piece 4 to the template**

▶ I have a portable ironing pad that rests on a small table next to my sewing table so that I can turn to the side and easily press each piece firmly in place before moving on to the next. The pads are available commercially, but you can make your own by draping a padded ironing board cover over a table. It's much quicker than getting up and walking to the ironing board after adding each patch.

▸ Courthouse Steps blocks are used to make the quilt Pitchers for Tildy's Cabin on my About.com Quilting Web site. Full and half foundation-pieced blocks surround nine appliquéd pitcher and bowl sets. You can make a miniature with 3½" blocks, or a small wall hanging with the 7" practice blocks. Visit http://about.com/quilting/pitchers quilt.

10. Flip the strip right-side up and check placement. If it's okay, even up the seam allowance and press piece 4 firmly in place.

11. Continue adding the rest of the pieces in the same way, working in numerical order. Sew dark pieces across from each other in the block and light pieces across from each other in the other direction. Be sure to trim up the seam allowance after each seam, otherwise you could end up with a bulky mass of fabric on the back of your quilt block. Check placement carefully after sewing a piece to the foundation.

12. The edges of outermost pieces should extend slightly past the line you drew on the template after it was enlarged. To finish the block, cut through all layers on that outermost line.

If you had fun making the Courthouse Steps block, make additional blocks and sew them together to create a quilt. Leave the papers in place until all blocks are sewn together.

Sometimes you'll assemble asymmetrical blocks. A block image is drawn on the front side of the template and fabric is applied to the back. That means each block is a mirror image of the drawn pattern. That doesn't matter when blocks are symmetrical—the same from side to side. But it makes a difference if a block's design is off center. Create a mirror-image template whenever you want to reverse a block image.

Here's how to cut patches for blocks with triangles. The practice block was made with squares and bars. They're the easiest shapes to foundation piece. If a block contains triangles, the pattern will very likely tell you to cut the triangles a bit larger than necessary, just to make sure you have plenty of extra fabric for seam allowances. You can usually reduce triangle sizes once you're familiar with the technique.

Use these foundation-piecing tips to help you make accurate and easy blocks. Once you've made a few foundation-pieced blocks you'll be ready to try more. They're all assembled in the same basic way, and most patterns you find will have pieces that are numbered to indicate sewing order. You'll develop favorite techniques of your own after a little practice, but these tips will help get you off to a quick start.

- Don't worry if the raw edges of patches don't match exactly when you position them to sew a seam. You can trim them back after sewing.
- Use a pair of tweezers to remove small pieces of temporary foundations. You'll find special long-handled tweezers at fabric stores.
- Make seam lines easier to see on the back of papers by sewing through them from the front with an unthreaded needle. Use long stitches to avoid perforating the paper so closely that it breaks away as you're sewing fabric to the template.
- Some blocks can be paper pieced in segments, which are then sewn together to complete the block.
- Change your needle often. Needles become dull quickly when they sew through bunches of paper and fabric.

Learn to String Piece

String piecing is a freeform type of foundation piecing. Long strips of fabric, called strings, are sewn to a plain piece of muslin or other fabric. The strings can be any width. Their widths can differ and

ELSEWHERE ON THE WEB

▶ Here's a fun string-pieced quilts gallery, provided by Quilt Town USA, publishers of quilting magazines. The gallery includes vintage and contemporary quilts, with background information about the quiltmakers. You'll find lots of excellent ideas at www.quilttownusa.com/ Quilt_Gallery/stringpieced gallery.htm.

they don't even have to be cut straight—angled strips make a string-pieced block even more charming.

String piecing is a "make do" technique, a way to use leftover scraps of fabric, but it's more common for today's quilters to buy yardage just so they can cut it up into strings. The string-pieced table runner in Chapter 11 will get you off to a good start with string piecing, but there are lots of other ways to make string-pieced blocks. We'll try a few more in this chapter. Read through Chapter 11 before you begin—just to get the basics down pat, then come back here to make a few practice blocks.

You can string piece from different angles. The table runner in Chapter 11 has string-pieced quilt blocks that are made by sewing fabric strips along a muslin square's diagonal. Try sewing them straight across the block, from one horizontal side to the other. Arrange the blocks in rows, with some strings pointing up and down and adjacent blocks with strings pointing to the sides.

Fig. 8-6 Strings sewn to the foundation horizontally

Try cutting string-pieced blocks apart once diagonally to make half-square triangles, then sew the triangles together in different configurations. Each triangle will finish at ⅞" less than the width on its short sides.

Sew a block where strings change direction. Mark a diagonal line from one corner to another on a square foundation. Sew strips perpendicular to the line, moving diagonally from one side to a corner and overlapping the line by about ¼". When that half of the block is pieced, change direction by placing a long strip right-side down across the ends of the first set of strips. Sew it in place and flip right-side up. Continue adding long strips next to it as you work to the corner of the block.

Fig. 8-7 **Sewing strings in different configurations**

Crazy-Quilting Basics

Crazy quilts are another type of foundation piecing where patches are sewn randomly to an unmarked piece of muslin or other fabric. Crazy quilting is similar to string piecing, but instead of long strings you'll use all sorts of patchwork shapes. The finished quilt is then adorned with lace, buttons, cording—any type of embellishment you choose.

Crazy quilts became popular in the late nineteen century. They were often smaller quilts used as throws, not bed quilts. You'll find vintage crazy quilts stitched from wools and cottons, but more luxurious fabrics such as velvet, silk, and satin were also popular.

Decorative embroidery stitches are commonly used along seams that separate patches, and also inside individual pieces, some-times to record a date or a name. Colorful silk cigar wrappers and souvenir ribbons were often worked into the design. Crazy quilts sometimes give us a personal glimpse into the life of the quiltmaker, not unlike the collage pieces we see in contemporary scrapbooks.

We have an endless number of fabrics to choose from, so our crazy quilts can have any look we desire. We can turn crazy quilts into special family mementos by sprinkling photographs throughout the blocks.

Think about creating your own special crazy-quilt stash. You might not make the quilt for awhile, but when you're ready it will be filled with fabrics and embellishments to incorporate in your quilt. Start collecting ribbons, laces, and buttons. Save tickets from a special event to scan into your computer and print on fabric. Tuck away copies of family photos. Add anything to the bin that will make your quilt a personal remembrance.

If you want to get started now, choose fabrics and cut foundations. You can piece a crazy quilt on a very large foundation, but the easiest way to get started is to use block-size squares and sew them together after each is finished. Cut squares or rectangles of muslin or nonwoven interfacing that are about 1" larger on each side than the size you want the blocks to finish at. Crazy quilting is random, so any size you choose is fine.

Select fabrics in an assortment of print scales, colors, and values. Use stripes, florals, geometric prints, plaids, and tone on tones to incorporate good visual texture within the quilt.

We'll piece this first block from slightly off center.

Here is how to start your crazy-quilt block:

1. Cut a piece of fabric with an odd number of edges—three, five, or seven is a good choice. Pin it right-side up slightly off center on your foundation.
2. Place another patch of fabric on top of the first, right-side down and aligned along one edge. The edges need not be the same length.

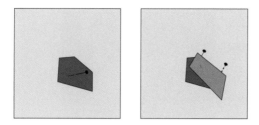

Fig. 8-8 **Start adding patches to the foundation**

3. Mark the endpoints of the piece underneath with straight pins if the second fabric stretches past them, then sew a ¼" seam between the pins to attach fabrics.
4. Flip the second piece right-side up and press in place. Trim the edges of the second patch so that they are aligned with the edges of the first.

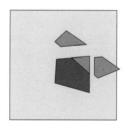

Fig. 8-9 **Trim edges of second piece**

5. Working clockwise, place a third fabric right-side down along the combined edges of the first and second patch, using pins again to mark the endpoints of the patches underneath. Sew with a ¼" seam. Flip the new patch up and trim its ends to match the combined edges of the first two patches.

Fig. 8-10 **Adding more patches to the block**

6. Continue adding more patches in the same way, making sure each new patch extends across the length of the patches underneath it. Keep working clockwise from the center outwards.
7. When the foundation is covered with fabric, press it thoroughly and trim it to the desired unfinished size. Repeat to make additional blocks, then sew blocks together into a quilt. Embellish as desired.

Camouflage seams where blocks are sewn together. The extra inch or so you added to the foundation's size makes it easy to camouflage seams where blocks are joined. Before you square up the block, fold back the edges of a few outer patches and pin them out of the way so they won't be cut. Sew blocks together, keeping those patches pinned out of the way so they won't be caught up in the seam allowance. Unpin and turn the patches right-side up. Fold the edges of the patches under and appliqué them to the adjacent block.

Here's a trick to help you break up long seams within the block. Patches sometimes become long and narrow as you add patches around the center of a block. Break up those long seams by sewing three fabrics together then adding them to the block as one unit.

There's an easy way to add curves to your crazy-quilt blocks. To add a curved shape, cut a curved patch with one straight side. Add the curved piece to the foundation, sewing along its straight edge. Flip the curve right-side up and use a pencil to mark around its edge. Flip it back again, right-side down, and add pieces to the foundation, extending their edges underneath and well inside the area of the marked curve. When the pieces have filled in the curve, turn the loose piece right-side up and appliqué its curved edge to the block, covering the edges of the fill-in patches.

Some quilters like to start piecing in a corner. Place your first patch in a corner and work clockwise to cover its inner edges. When you reach the last portion of the edge, turn and work counterclockwise. Add more patches to the square using the same back and forth motion.

Adorn your crazy quilt with any type of embroidery or other embellishment you desire. Use your sewing machine to add decorative stitches if hand embroidery is not your favorite technique. Sew on laces, silk ribbon, and cording. Sprinkle decorative buttons across the quilt.

Most vintage crazy quilts were tied rather than quilted. You can use thin batting between the quilt blocks and backing if you like, but the foundation might provide plenty of depth all on its own.

ELSEWHERE ON THE WEB

▶ The State Museum of Pennsylvania's Web site includes an interesting photograph from the back of an English paper pieced quilt. The photo shows a close-up portion of the quilt back. You can see how hexagons were basted to the papers—which appear to be a combination of printed matter and personal letters. Visit www.statemuseumpa.org/quilts05new/pages/glossary/9english.htm.

English Paper Piecing

English paper piecing isn't the same type of foundation piecing you've read about in this chapter, but you do use paper foundations to help you assemble the quilt. For English paper piecing you'll cut a paper pattern for every piece in the quilt, then baste fabric to the pattern pieces before sewing them together. Like other paper foundations, the papers remain in the quilt until adjacent patches are sewn together.

The traditional Grandmother's Flower Garden is made from continuous hexagons and is nearly always paper pieced. It's a good pattern to practice with. Choose scraps of four different fabrics: a dark, a medium, a medium light, and a light. Cut thirty-seven hexagons from cardstock or another heavy paper. Use the hexagon template, Figure 8-11. You can enlarge the template to any size desired.

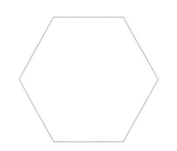

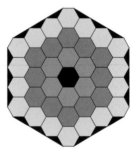

Fig. 8-11 **Hexagon template**

Fig. 8-12 **Grandmother's Flower Garden block**

Here is how to practice English paper piecing:

1. Quick-cut fabric hexagons that are ½" larger than your paper shapes. Cut one dark, twelve medium, six medium light, and eighteen light fabric hexagons.

2. Center a paper hexagon on the reverse side of a fabric hexagon. Pin the two together. Fold the fabric edges over the paper and use a hand-sewing needle and long running stitch to baste them in place. Repeat to baste all fabrics to paper hexagons.

3. Knot your thread at one end. Align the dark patch with a medium light patch, placing right sides together. Holding the patches in place, insert the needle through the folds of the edges along one side, catching the fabric with the needle but not sewing into the paper. Pull the needle through the fabrics and then repeat, inserting it again from the same direction, very close to the first stitch. Continue sewing to complete the seam.

TOOLS YOU NEED

▶ Cutting out all those paper templates can be a chore— and hard on your rotary cutter. Paper Pieces offers precut paper patterns in just about any shape and size you can imagine. The pieces will all be exactly alike, and that enhances the accuracy of your quilt. You'll find templates to help you make all sorts of paper pieced quilts at www.paperpieces.com.

Fig. 8-13 **Sewing hexagons together**

4. Align a second medium light patch along the next side of the dark hexagon and sew together using the same technique, called a whipstitch. Align the adjacent edges of the two medium light patches and sew them together.

5. Continue adding the medium light patches to the dark center patch. Follow up with a row of medium patches and then finish by surrounding that row with light patches.

You'll see that the block you just made has jagged edges around its perimeter. You can fill those in by cutting partial templates and basting fabric to them before sewing them to the block. You can also turn under the edges of the outer hexagons and appliqué the block to a large piece of fabric.

If you would like to use the block, make a throw pillow from it. You'll find instructions to make a pillow in Chapter 14.

Get Linked

You'll find more resources about all kinds of foundation piecing on my About.com Quilting Web site.

STRING PIECING IDEAS

Read more tips and techniques about string piecing, including methods you can use to cut patchwork shapes from long segments of string pieced fabric.

http://about.com/quilting/stringpiecing

PRINTING ON FABRIC

Learn how to print pictures and patterns on your inkjet printer.

http://about.com/quilting/printingonfabric

CRAZY-QUILTING TIPS

The look of your crazy quilt can change dramatically when you apply embroidery, lace, cording, and other types of embellishments. This is where you'll find the tools you need to get started.

http://about.com/quilting/crazyquilts

Chapter 9

Finishing Up the Quilt

How Will You Quilt the Quilt?

Your quilt top is complete now, but it's not a quilt until you sandwich it with batting and backing, and then quilt and bind it. You might want to sew on a hanging sleeve to make it easy to display the quilt in a show or on a wall. Another finishing touch to consider is adding an identification label to the back of the quilt that documents when it was made and who made it. Finishing up is an important part of the quiltmaking process, so take as much time as you need to work through these last few details.

Quilting is one of the last things you'll do before finishing your project, but there are a few in-between steps that you can't take until you've decided how you want to quilt it. If you want to hand quilt it with intricate motifs, they'll probably need to be drawn on the quilt before it is sandwiched with batting and backing. It's much easier to trace and draw on fabric with a hard surface behind it than it is to mark on a soft object with batting and backing under it.

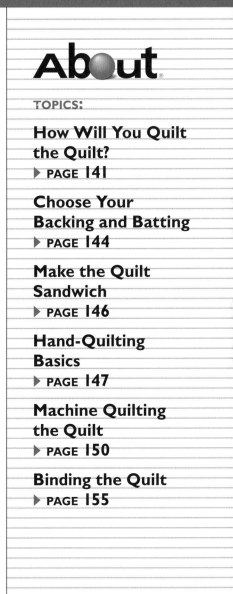

About

Machine quilters sometimes don't mark for quilting at all, opting instead to use techniques that allow them to quilt the piece without any guides. You'll be ready to move on to other finishing tasks as soon as you've considered your quilting options and prepped the quilt if necessary.

TOOLS YOU NEED

▶ You'll need different tools for each portion of the finishing process. Read through the chapter to learn about the wide variety of options for marking your quilt before quilting it, for details about machine quilting versus hand quilting, and for a list of tools that will help you complete the quilt.

There are many ways to mark a quilt for any type of quilting. Traditionally, quilters used a sharp pencil with hard lead, usually designated by an H on the shaft, to mark quilting motifs onto their quilts. Mechanical pencils are a good marking choice because their leads always remain the same width. Several companies produce mechanical pencils made especially for quilters, with fine lead that's fairly easy to remove when the quilt is complete.

Some quilters use soapstone markers to draw their quilting motifs. The lines are easier to remove than lead but stay in place long enough to quilt the piece. Colored artist's pencils are another choice, but don't use them without testing the lines on scrap fabric to make sure they are not permanent. There are numerous types of specialty markers with lines that disappear when they are touched by water. Some marker lines disappear after being exposed to air for varying times. Investigate all types of markers and ask quilt shop staff and other quilters for personal recommendations.

Decide how you want to transfer quilting lines onto the quilt. You can find quilting designs all around you. Look at large fabric prints. Are there outlines within the print that would make wonderful quilting motifs? Place tracing paper over the fabric and use a dark, permanent marker to transfer the design to paper. If the designs aren't real visible, use a commercial light table under the layers or place them on top of a glass table and turn a short table lamp on underneath it.

Transfer the designs to the lighter colored areas of your quilt in the same way—by placing the drawing under the quilt and tracing it with your choice of marker. For dark fabrics, trace the design onto template plastic and use a craft knife to cut out channels that you can mark through.

Make freezer paper templates. Draw the outline of a shape onto the nonshiny side of freezer paper and cut out. Press the freezer paper in place on the quilt and quilt around it. Remove the shape and use again. You can construct a series of shapes to quilt within or around the first.

Commercial quilting patterns are available in books. Tear-away products are sold for machine quilting—follow the marked lines to quilt with your machine, then tear the paper away when you're finished. Quilt shops and fabric stores carry a wide assortment of precut plastic quilting stencils. Just lay the stencil on top of the quilt and run a marker through the lines to establish lines on your quilt. Quilters and quilt related companies offer new quilting patterns and techniques every year to make it easy for us to quilt our projects.

It's not necessary to premark some types of quilting lines. Outline quilting is a popular technique and is usually done by quilting ¼" outward from patches or appliqué shapes. Quarter-inch quilter's masking tape makes it easy to keep stitches straight. Position the tape around the shape and quilt along its edge. Remove the tape and reuse it when you're ready to move on to another area.

In-the-ditch quilting is done alongside a seam or the edge of an appliqué shape. Echo quilting sometimes follows in-the-ditch quilting and is made up of a series of quilting lines that start at a piece of patchwork or appliqué and radiate outward at regular intervals.

Stipple quilting is made up of closely spaced, curved lines that wander across the quilt's surface. They can come close to each

TOOLS YOU NEED

▶ Chalk pencils are another marking choice and are available in many styles. Chalk pouncers, loosely woven bags filled with chalk that are blotted up and down through open channels in templates, are another option. Pounced chalk is best used after the quilt is sandwiched with batting and backing, and just before quilting each area, because chalk lines tend to rub off with handling. Keep in mind that chalk from markers is a little more durable.

other, but they do not touch. **Meander quilting** is similar, but lines are spaced further apart. Both are freehand methods that can be done by hand or machine.

If you want to premark extensive quilting lines, do it now before you move on to the next step.

Choose Your Backing and Batting

A quilt has three layers: the top that you spent so much time creating, a thicker layer called batting that gives the quilt depth, and a final layer of fabric called the backing. The three layers are generally referred to as the **quilt sandwich**. You have a few more choices to make before you can put the sandwich together and move on.

Consider which batting material will work best for your quilt. Battings fall into two very broad categories: natural and synthetic. From that point the huge number of selections can be confusing for a beginning quilter. Cotton, wool, and silk battings are made from natural fibers. Polyester is a synthetic. You'll also find quilt batting that's a combination of natural and synthetic materials—usually polyester and cotton.

Pure cotton is a traditional batting choice. Some types of cotton batting are very dense, which makes them more difficult to hand quilt than others. Battings that are labeled "needle-punched" have been processed in a way that helps break up cotton fibers to allow easier hand quilting. Polyester batting and batting made from a blend of polyester and cotton are typically easier to hand quilt than 100 percent cotton batting.

Some cotton battings must be quilted closely so that fibers don't pull apart during use and during a wash, but newer batting assembly methods allow you to safely place stitches farther apart. Check the batting's label for quilting and care instructions.

There's evidence that polyester batting will disintegrate over time. If you are making an heirloom quilt, most quilting professionals recommend that you use pure cotton batting as a filler for your quilt. Polyester batting is prone to **bearding**, which means that fibers migrate through the quilt top and backing and become visible on the surfaces of the quilt.

Loft is another batting characteristic to consider. The term refers to the height—or depth—of the batting. A thin, low loft batting gives your quilt a vintage or traditional appearance. A thick, high loft batting is a great choice for comforters or other projects that you want to have a puffy appearance.

Decide how you want to make the quilt backing. The back side of the quilt can be made from one fabric, or it can be pieced from two or more fabrics. Some quilts are even fully reversible, with a completed quilt top on each side. Several fabric manufacturers are producing wide backing fabrics that allow you to use a single panel of fabric on the reverse side of your quilts instead of piecing together panels of typical 42"–44" wide fabric.

Choose any fabric you wish for the backing. It can match or blend with the fabrics used on the front of your quilt, or it can be totally different. Some quilters choose a backing fabric especially for its print, and then quilt from the back, following the lines in the printed fabric.

To make a wide backing, you must piece together panels of fabric that are normal width.

Here is how to measure and assemble the backing:

1. Measure the finished quilt top horizontally and vertically. Add 4" to each measurement for a small wall hanging and 8" to each measurement for a large quilt.

ASK YOUR GUIDE

Where can I find quilting designs?

▶ You can find lots of free quilting designs online by searching for the term quilting designs on Google or another search engine. Quilting patterns are available commercially in books and as plastic templates with channels that are precut to make the design easy to trace. Quilting magazines often include motifs that can be enlarged to suit your quilt, and tear-away designs are readily available for machine quilters.

▶ When you think of quilt batting you might think of a thick, white substance, but batting is available in other colors. Some batting is neutral in color, or unbleached. You'll also find gray and black batting. Dark batting is suitable for a quilt made from darker fabrics. Neutral works well with quilts made from lighter fabrics or a combination that includes light fabrics.

2. Decide if you want backing panels to be pieced vertically or horizontally.
3. Remove the selvages from both edges of your fabric. Measure the remaining fabric width.
4. Determine how many panels are required to make a backing that measures the dimensions calculated in step 1. Cut panels that are 1" wider than the required size and sew them together with a ½" seam allowance. Press seams open.

Make the Quilt Sandwich

Now it's time to put your layers together and finish the quilt. What I'll describe to you is a traditional method to assemble the layers, but there are many different opinions on the sandwich making process. Everyone has a favorite method and everyone develops little tricks to handle the layers efficiently. Ask questions when you talk to quilters about their methods and try to read as many articles and patterns as possible about the topic. In time you will develop your own favorite techniques to finish a quilt.

Here is how to finish your quilt by making the quilt sandwich:

1. Lay your backing right-side down on a smooth, flat surface. Some quilters like to pull the edges of the backing taut and hold them in place with pieces of masking tape. Others prefer to leave the edges free and simply make sure the backing remains nice and flat while working with it.
2. Prepare your batting following the manufacturer's instructions. Center it on top of the backing and smooth it out.
3. Center your quilt top right-side up on the batting and smooth it gently to eliminate folds.
4. If you plan to hand quilt, use a darning needle and white thread to baste the layers together, placing long stitches through all three layers. White thread is a good choice since

it has no colors to rub off onto your quilt. Stitching lines should be close enough to keep the layers from shifting during final assembly but not so close that they'll get in the way of your quilting stitches.

Machine quilters do not baste the quilt with stitches. Instead, they use rustproof safety pins to hold the layers together, placing pins 3"–5" apart through all layers. Position all of the pins, and then go back and close them all at once. Quilting suppliers sell specially made basting pins that are bent along their length. The slight bend makes the pins easier to insert and remove.

Hand-Quilting Basics

Hand quilting is usually done after placing your quilt in some sort of frame to keep it from shifting around as you work. The frame can be large enough to hold the entire quilt, or it can be a smaller hoop that holds only a portion of the quilt at a time. Some quilters never use a quilting frame; they simply hold the quilts in their laps as they work.

Large floor frames hold a full-size quilt. No basting is required—the sides of the frames have devices to secure the layers while you quilt. Roller frames allow you to work on larger portions of the quilt at one time. They don't require as much floor space as floor frames. Round or oval hoops are much smaller. Some hoops are on floor stands. Others are small enough to rest comfortably in your lap.

Hand quilters should think about finger protection. You'll need to use a thimble on the hand that works on top of the quilt. The thimble helps you push the needle down through the quilt's layers. A finger of the hand that rests underneath the quilt is used to detect the needle when it emerges. If you don't shield it, the

▶ Special tools are available to help keep your fingers from becoming sore as you close the safety pins. Do you have a serrated grapefruit spoon? Use that instead of a special tool by placing the shaft of a pin within one of the little notches. Push on the spoon to close the pin.

finger will become calloused from repeated pinpricks. Commercial shields are available. They are typically adhesive backed dots of a sheer material that allows you to feel the needle but doesn't let it pierce your finger. A few layers of masking tape will also do the trick.

Decide which types of needles and thread you want to use. Hand quilters use short but sturdy needles called betweens. Regular hand-sewing needles are more likely to bend when you quilt with them, because it's sometimes difficult to push the needle through several layers of fabric and batting.

Use hand-quilting thread when possible because it is stronger than all-purpose thread. If you must use an all-purpose thread, coat it with beeswax to make it more durable and keep it from tangling. Beeswax is available at most quilt shops. Like fabric, thread has a grain, and it will flow through your fabric more easily in one direction than the other. Take advantage of that characteristic by knotting the end of the thread that came off the spool last.

You'll need to practice the quilting stitch. The quilting stitch isn't difficult to do, but it does take practice. The best thing you can do is attend a class where a teacher will show you how to do the stitch in person, or attend a quilt show where members are demonstrating their quilting skills. You'll discover that experienced quilters are nearly always happy to teach newcomers a few tricks.

Remember one more thing: everyone quilts a bit differently. Use the instructions as a general guide, but don't hesitate to change the technique a bit to make it work for you.

Here is how to practice the quilting stitch:

1. Thread a between with about 18" of hand-quilting thread. Knot the thread by wrapping the thread's tail around the

▶ Hand-sewing needle size decreases as numerical designations increase, so a size 9 needle is larger than a 10. Although small needles help you keep stitches shorter, start with a 9 or 10 and graduate to a 12 after you have a bit of hand-quilting experience. Needle sizes do vary a bit by manufacturer and country of origin, so experiment with different needles until you find one you like.

needle a few times, then pulling the needle through the wrap while holding them with your fingers. Keep pulling and the wraps will form a knot at the end of the thread.

2. Insert the needle through the top of the quilt about an inch from where you want to start quilting. Move the needle into the batting but do not go through the backing. Pull the needle back up directly on a quilting line and tug gently to pop the knot through the quilt and bury it in the batting.

3. Align the needle so that it is perpendicular to the surface of the quilt. Move it downward with the thimble just until you feel the sharp tip emerge underneath the quilt. Now push upwards to bring the tip back to the top of the quilt. Move downward again to take another stitch. Take several stitches using the same rocking motion, then pull on the needle to move the thread through the stitches. Repeat to sew more quilting stitches.

4. To end a line of stitching, bring the needle up through the fabric just past the last stitch, forming a loop about ¼" from the surface of the quilt. Pull the needle through the loop to create a knot, and then insert the needle back into the quilt where the thread is emerging. Bring the needle back up through the quilt about an inch away and tug to pop the knot into the batting. Cut the thread at the quilt top.

There might be times you would prefer to hand tie a quilt. Hand tying is a quick way to finish a quilt. Ties are single stitches that are taken through all layers of a quilt at regular intervals. It's a perfect method to use when you make a puffy comforter that's filled with high-loft batting, because the loft will billow out at every tie. It's easier to finish a foundation-pieced quilt with lots of layers, like the string-pieced table runner in Chapter 11.

Here is how to hand tie a quilt:

1. Sandwich the quilt and baste it with safety pins or straight pins.
2. Thread a darning needle with a long strand of perle cotton. You can also use yarn or multiple strands of embroidery floss.
3. Beginning at the top of the quilt, take a stitch through all layers. Bring the needle back up through the layers very near the first stitch and pull the thread through until you have a tail that's 3"–4" long.
4. Move about 4" from the first tie and take another stitch through all layers. Bring the needle back up through the layers, taking care to leave loose thread between the stitches. Continue taking stitches about every 4".
5. When you run out of thread, cut the thread between stitches in half. Tie tails together at each stitch with two square knots. Trim the tails to any length desired.
6. Thread another needle and add more ties until the surface is covered with equally spaced ties—or tie in a decorative arrangement.

Machine Quilting the Quilt

Not too many years ago it was somewhat rare to see machine-quilted quilts in the awards circle at quilt shows. That's no longer true. Machine quilting has evolved into a true art form, and many of the quilts receiving top honors at highly competitive shows throughout the world have been quilted by machine instead of by hand. Entire books have been written about machine quilting, so please treat this text as an introduction. It's another technique you'll learn best by experimentation. Machine-quilting techniques

shades of the past in batiks

BY MELISSA HARRIS, LONGARM MACHINE QUILTED BY AMI KRENZEL

BY COLLENE RUSSELL

basket wall hanging

string-pieced table runner

BY KRISTEN RENNEKER

string-pieced table runner

rag quilt

BY COLENE RUSSELL

BY JANET WICKELL

basket throw pillow
with yo-yo flowers

fabric reproductions

BY JANET WICKELL

UNQUILTED TOP BY JULI LEVINE

**rag-edged
denim purse**

shades of the past

miniature paisley stars

string-pieced table runner

BY JANET WICKELL

rag quilt

and innovations are changing rapidly. If you find that it's a method you enjoy, be sure to keep up with the trends. Read about machine quilting online. Look closely at machine-quilted pieces in shows, books, and magazines. Even the quilts you don't particularly like will help you, because you'll see things you definitely don't want to repeat in your own quilts.

You can machine quilt with all types of threads. There's no shortage of thread choices for machine quilters, and there are only a few types of thread that you should not use. Do not machine quilt with hand-quilting thread that's coated with any type of substance to make it stiff, because the coating could damage your sewing machine. Avoid nylon thread that feels as thick as fishing line. It isn't attractive, it will damage your fabrics, and it will become brittle and break very easily.

Let the character of your project guide your thread selection. If you're making a very traditional quilt, cotton quilting threads that mimic hand quilting might be your best choice. If the project is an art quilt or other contemporary piece it might look wonderful quilted with variegated or metallic threads.

We don't see it as often as we did a few years ago, but some quilters use a very fine nylon thread to machine quilt. It isn't like the fishing line thread I mentioned earlier in the chapter—this thread is finer than hair. Quilting stitches made with the thread are visible as indentations, but individual stitches aren't as apparent. The thread is available in clear and smoke-colored versions.

Balancing your sewing machine's tension and keeping threads intact can be difficult when you sew with decorative threads that break easily or aren't as smooth as regular quilting threads. Poor tension is a pesky little problem that leads to looped stitches on either the front or back of the quilt. Ideally, stitches on each side of the machine should be nicely formed and even.

Use 100 percent cotton thread in the bobbin and your decorative thread through the needle. Perform a stitching test and check for tension problems. If the top thread is looped or very visible on the back of the piece, make the top tension a bit tighter. If your bobbin threads are visible on the front, make the top tension weaker or the bobbin tension stronger. Read your sewing machine manual to learn how to adjust tension settings.

Start each project with a suitable machine needle. It's a good idea to use a sewing needle made especially for machine quilting. These needles have larger eyes that threads can move through without being stripped or broken as easily as they would be when threaded through a normal sewing needle with a small eye.

Machine-quilting needles are made from a metal that helps them stay cooler than typical needles do when they move up and down at a rapid rate through the layers of a quilt, another characteristic that minimizes breakage. You can also machine quilt with machine embroidery needles, which have even slightly larger eyes to accommodate decorative threads.

Use a walking foot if you plan to do a lot of straight machine quilting. A walking foot is a special presser foot with a mechanism that grips the top layer of the quilt and advances it through the machine in synch with the feed dogs, the jagged little metal plates that grasp the bottom of the quilt to help move it along under the needle.

Most sewing machine manufacturers make a walking foot for their machines. Sewing accessory companies also offer generic versions that might fit your sewing machine.

Practice your straight quilting stitches. Straight-line quilting is appropriate for in-the-ditch quilting, outline quilting, and grid quilting. Practice the technique by sandwiching an 18" square of top fabric with a matching piece of batting and backing. There's no need to mark the sample piece with quilting lines.

Here is how to practice your straight quilting stitches:

1. Baste the layers with a few safety pins. Put your walking foot on and thread the needle with cotton thread.
2. Place the sample under the walking foot and take one stitch. Lift the presser foot and tug on the top thread to bring a loop of the bobbin thread to the top surface of the sample. Use tweezers or a straight pin to grab the loop and pull the thread all the way through to the top. Don't neglect this step or the thread could get mixed in with stitches on the reverse side of the sample, creating a messy seam line.
3. Take six to ten very short stitches, and then gradually lengthen the stitches to the desired length. Sew about halfway across the square and begin to gradually shorten stitches, taking six to ten very short stitches again.
4. Remove the sample from the machine. Trim threads on the top and bottom flush with the fabric. The small stitches will keep threads from unraveling.
5. Begin sewing again—you're just practicing so it doesn't matter what type of lines you quilt. Try stopping with the needle in the sample and pivot the piece to stitch in another direction.

You can get a feel for quilting in the ditch with a machine by making a sample from six 4" squares assembled into two rows. Sandwich it with backing and batting and sew along seam lines, staying as close to the seam as possible. Sew on the low side of the seam—the side without a seam allowance under it. That isn't always possible when you're sewing a real quilt block, but it provides the best results.

Now try free-motion machine quilting. Free-motion machine quilting is done using a special quilting presser foot. It resembles a darning foot, which has only a round hole for the needle to pass through, but the hole in a quilting foot is much larger. Quilt with the darning foot that came with your sewing machine if you do not have a free-motion quilting foot.

Always put the feed dogs down during free-motion quilting. Refer to your sewing machine manual if you aren't sure how to do that. Feed dogs aren't needed to guide fabric under the presser foot and will be in the way if left up. You control the stitch length by moving the fabric and running the foot pedal. Free-motion quilting takes some practice, but you can achieve beautiful results once you've mastered the technique.

Here is how to practice free-motion quilting:

1. Make a sample quilt sandwich from a large-scale printed fabric. Place the feed dogs in the down position. Take one stitch and pull the bobbin thread to the top, just as you did for straight machine quilting.
2. Place your hands on each side of the sample quilt and press down the sewing machine's foot control. Move the sample slightly to take several very short stitches.
3. Continue to move the sample under the needle. Stitch length depends on how quickly you move the sample and how fast you run the foot pedal. Try to work at an even speed.
4. Try quilting on some of the printed lines of your fabric.
5. Stop sewing by taking several very small stitches again, then cutting threads as you did for straight quilting.

Those five steps are a very basic look at a complex technique. Your first stitches will be uneven and jagged. You probably discovered that it was very difficult to follow a printed line. That's normal, so don't worry about it. Free-motion machine quilting typically takes a great deal of practice to master. Keep working on it and you'll soon begin to see a difference in your quilting stitches.

Binding the Quilt

Binding's functional purpose is to cover the raw edges of the quilt sandwich, but it can be used to frame the quilt with one last design element. The binding can blend or contrast with the quilt top and borders, and it can be narrow or wide. It can even be made from multiple fabrics for a patchwork look.

The binding we'll use in this book is called continuous double-fold binding, also sometimes known as French binding. The finished binding is two layers of fabric deep on the front and back sides of the quilt. You can sew a single layer of fabric around the quilt edges if you prefer, but I do not recommend that method for anything other than wall hangings and miniature quilts. One layer of fabric is more likely to wear away in quilts that are used and laundered as the rough inner layers constantly rub against it. An extra layer of fabric keeps the binding intact longer.

Crosswise-grain strips are a good choice for binding straight quilt edges. The grain isn't usually absolutely straight, so it moves at just a bit of an angle across the strips from front to back—not straight up and down them. If a single thread becomes weak and breaks from use, it's unlikely that the damaged thread would create a rip along the entire length of the binding. Crosswise strips are also stretchy enough to wind around large curves.

Square up your quilt edges before you make and sew on binding. Quilt edges sometimes get a bit out of square during the quilting process, particularly at corners. Place a large square ruler at each corner of your quilt. Are edges skewed or uneven? If they are, move the backing and batting out of the way and carefully trim just the quilt top so that its corners are at right angles to each other. The excess batting and backing will be trimmed after you sew on the binding.

Squaring up is a bit tricky if your quilt doesn't have borders. Be careful not to cut into the quarter-inch seam allowance of blocks that are on the quilt's edges.

Wavy edges can sometimes be fixed by sewing a long basting stitch along wavy sides of the quilt, then gathering those edges just a little to pull them into shape. Don't overdo it or the edges could end up looking ruffled!

Determine how much binding you need and assemble the strips. Measure your quilt along its top and its bottom and multiply that figure by two. Add 14" to the total to determine how long the continuous binding strip must be. To make long strips you'll sew crosswise-grain strips together until you have one long binding strip.

To help determine strip width, use this formula:

(2 × finished binding width + seam allowance) × 2

Let's use a ¼" binding as an example:
(2 × ¼" + ¼") × 2
(¾") × 2 = 1½"

Unless I am making a small quilt with very thin batting, I always add ½" to the figure to allow for batting depth and to give me a little extra width when I fold the binding to the back of the quilt. Some quilters add even more width to their strips.

Here is how to assemble your strips:

1. Place two 2" × 42" fabric strips right sides together, perpendicular to each other. Let the ends overlap each other as shown in Figure 9-1. Hold the strip ends together with a straight pin.

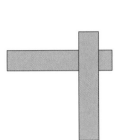

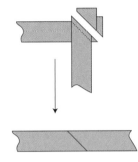

Fig. 9-1 **Align binding strip edges**   Fig. 9-2 **Sew and trim strips**

2. Mark the top strip on the diagonal, beginning and ending the line at the inward corner where the two strips intersect each other. Sew the strips together on the marked line. Trim away the excess fabric, leaving about a ¼" seam. Press the seam allowance open.
3. Trim off the triangular nubs that extend past the sides of the strip.
4. Sew additional strips together until you have assembled the length of binding required for your quilt.
5. Press the strip in half lengthwise, wrong sides together and matching raw edges.

Sew the binding to your quilt. It's easy to sew the binding to your quilt in one long piece with neatly mitered corners. Just follow these simple steps—you're almost finished.

Do I really have to sew a diagonal seam? Sewing the strips end to end would be easier.

▶ Sewing strips together with butted ends creates very bulky and unattractive seams when the binding strips are folded in half and then sewn to the quilt. Diagonal seams flow down the length of the binding, so they are easier to work with and aren't as noticeable in the finished quilt.

1. Starting about a third of the distance between two corners of the quilt, align the raw edge of one end of the binding with the edge of the quilt top.

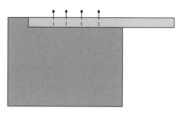

Fig. 9-3 **Pin binding to quilt edge**

2. Leave the beginning 3"–4" of binding unpinned, then pin several inches of the binding to the quilt. Without pinning, stretch the rest of the strip around the sides of the quilt to make sure no seam allowances in the binding will end up sewn in a corner to create excess bulk. If you discover a corner that will be marred with a binding seam, reposition the binding and check again.

3. Sew the binding to the quilt with a ¼" seam allowance, leaving the beginning tail free. Stop sewing ¼" before the approaching quilt edge. Backstitch, cut threads, and remove the quilt from the sewing machine.

4. Fold the unsewn binding tail straight up, with its right edge parallel to the side of the quilt you'll bind next. Manipulate the strip so that it forms a 45-degree angle on its lower edge.

5. Fold the binding down, placing the top of the fold flush with the edge of the quilt behind it. Align raw edges with the side of the quilt.

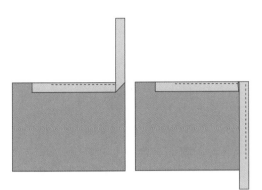

Fig. 9-4 **Mitering a corner of the binding**

6. Pin the quilt binding to the entire side of the quilt. Start sewing ¼" inward, where the last seam ended. Backstitch, then begin sewing forward again, ending the seam ¼" from the edge of the quilt as you did on the first side. Backstitch.

7. Remove the quilt from the machine and miter the corner as you did the first. Sew remaining sides in the same way.

8. On the last side, end the seam 4"–6" from the original starting point. Backstitch.

9. Trim excess binding, but leave a tail that's long enough to overlap the unsewn tail on the beginning end by about 4".

10. Unfold the beginning tail and make a 45-degree cut at its end. Open the ending tail and place it alongside the beginning tail. Mark a line where the two meet. Add a ½" seam allowance past the marked line, toward the end of the ending tail. Trim excess fabric past the line.

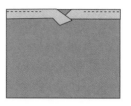

Fig. 9-5 Mark and trim binding ends

11. Place the angled tails right sides together, offsetting their ends by ¼". Sew the ends together with a ¼" seam allowance.

12. Refold the quilt binding, then pin and sew the remaining binding edge to the quilt.

13. Carefully trim all layers of the quilt to match the binding's seam allowance. Trimming after adding the binding ensures that your bound edges will be consistent—filled with batting to their edges.

Sew the binding to the back of the quilt. Now you'll fold the binding to the back of the quilt and sew it in place to finish the piece. Some quilters like to fold the binding as they work. If you secure edges with straight pins, work with only a short distance at a time. Otherwise your threads will get caught up in the pins, and I guarantee the pins will poke you! Special binding clips are available to hold the edges in place. They're made exactly like metal barrettes that spring open and shut at their centers.

Here is how to sew the binding to the back of the quilt:

1. Starting along any side, take the edge of the binding to the back side of the quilt, where it will cover the seam used to attach the binding.

2. Use a blind stitch to sew the edge of the binding to the backing. Use a thread that matches or blends with the binding. Be careful not to let stitches travel to the front of the quilt.
3. Sew all the way around the quilt, folding corners into miters on the front and back as you near them.

This method is one way to bind a quilt. There are numerous others, so take some time to read as many methods as possible as you become more experienced. I do have one important caution for you: Your seam allowance should match the finished width of your binding, and if you miter corners you must stop sewing seams that same distance from a corner—not ¼". Follow that simple rule and your corner miters will be perfect every time.

Read the directions in Chapter 10 if you would like to add a hanging sleeve to your quilt.

Get Linked

Visit the About.com Quilting site to learn many more quilt finishing techniques.

EASY ALTERNATIVE FOR BINDING ENDS

Here's another way to end binding strips where they come together. Some quilters think it's a quicker method.

http://about.com/quilting/easybinding

QUILTING YOUR QUILT

Find additional tips and tutorials to help you hand or machine quilt your project.

http://about.com/quilting/quiltingthequilt

FINISHING OPTIONS

This is the place to go to learn about the many other binding methods that can be used to finish a quilt, to make a quilt label, and to read about lots of other quilt finishing options.

http://about.com/quilting/finishingsteps

Chapter 10

Miniature Paisley Stars Quilt

Introduction to the Star Quilt

Miniature quilts are quick to make and they use just a little fabric. Minis make wonderful gifts, and your nonquilting friends will be impressed that you can make a quilt with such small pieces of fabric. Working small really isn't difficult at all when you sew accurate seams and press correctly—and you learned how to do that earlier in the book. Choose a favorite fabric for this little quilt, then go in search of a few more that will bring out its best features.

I love paisley fabrics and collect most every one I see, old and new. I know you've seen paisleys, because they've been popular forever. They are printed with teardrop shaped motifs that are decorated inside and out with flowers, geometrics, and lots of other shapes. I wanted to use a specific paisley fabric in my mini, and wanted it to stand out, but the print scale was too large. We wouldn't have been able to see the paisley shapes at all if I had cut it into small pieces for blocks.

▶ The Electric Quilt company features ideas for fireplace mantle toppers on its Web site. You'll find over 100 ideas, something for every season. The toppers can also be used as quilted valances or to hang from a shelf. Electric Quilt is a computer drawing program designed especially for quilters. Visit www.electricquilt.com/Albums/05/0509/0509p1.asp.

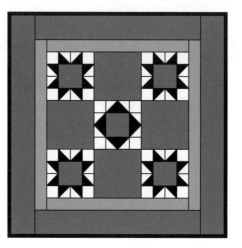

Fig. 10-1 Miniature Paisley Stars layout

My solution was to use the paisley for larger patches in the outer border and alternate blocks—plain squares of fabric that are used to separate the pieced quilt blocks. I chose a vintage looking pictorial fabric for the center of each star block and surrounded the squares with half-square triangle units to form stars in the outer rows. I flip-flopped the units to create a different design in the center block. You'll find a photo of this little quilt in the book's color insert.

Change the theme of this little miniature quilt any way you like to make it match any décor or event. It would be perfect for Christmas prints—maybe with Santa and his helpers used in block centers, or brightly colored winter birds filling those areas. Stitch one in fall colors to signify harvest or Halloween. Or maybe make a quilt for the Fourth of July, sewn in red, white, and blue, with stripes in the borders and stars in the center squares. No matter which theme you choose, you'll only need five fabrics to make this little quilt.

Finished quilt size: 15½" x 15½"

FABRIC REQUIREMENTS

Fabric	Yardage
Paisley	¼ yard
Light, inner border	⅛ yard
Light, star backgrounds	3⁄16 yard
Dark, star tips and binding	⅓ yard
Pictorial fabric for star centers	⅛ yard*

*The minimum most shops will cut.

CUTTING CHART

Fabric	Patch Size	Number Required
Paisley	3½" x 16" strip	1 (reserve remainder for border)
Light, inner border	Cut after assembly	
Light, star backgrounds	1¼" x 26" strip 1⅝" x 36" strip	1 1
Dark, star tips	1⅝" x 36" strip	1 (reserve remainder for binding)
Pictorial	2" x 2" squares	5

It's easy to sew small pieces if you follow a few simple guidelines. Some quilters hesitate to sew small blocks because they aren't real confident about their cutting and sewing accuracy. It's true, little errors are more obvious in a small quilt, but if you're cutting patches accurately, sewing a quarter-inch seam and taking care to press as you go, your blocks should be just fine. Use these tips to avoid problems with your miniature quilts.

▶ The pictorial centers of this little block would be a perfect place to display photos printed on fabric with your inkjet printer. You can scan photos or upload them to your computer from a digital camera. You can print directly on cloth or print to a sheet of paper that allows you to iron the image onto fabric. You'll find instructions to help you print on cloth at the About.com Quilting Web site. Visit http://about.com/quilting/fabricdyeing.

- It's best to stick with one brand of rulers throughout any project, especially when the project is a miniature. Slight differences in rulers and their marked lines can result in differences in your cut patches.
- Spray fabric with starch before cutting it. There's no need to make it as stiff as paper, but taking out the floppiness makes fabric easier to make accurate cuts.
- Thin batting is more appropriate for miniatures and wall hangings than a thick, puffy material. The low loft will help the quilt lay flatter wherever it's displayed, on a wall or draped across a piece of furniture.

You can use miniature quilts all throughout the house. You won't use them to cover beds, but miniature quilts can give any room a decorative boost. They do make wonderful gifts, but I think you'll want to make a few minis for yourself once you brainstorm a few ways to use them in your own home.

- The most obvious way to use minis is to hang them on a wall, just like a framed picture.
- Try draping a mini across the back of a chair or in the center of your sofa.
- Use a miniature quilt on a table, under a centerpiece.
- Hang one or more miniature quilts from a mini wooden quilt rack.
- Drape a mini over the top of a china cabinet, letting a portion of it hang down along the cabinet's side.
- Make a long miniature quilt and use it as a topper for your fireplace mantle.

Walk around the house and pay attention to places where you could use a bit of color and texture to liven things up. Those are the areas where a small quilt might be the perfect solution.

Make the Star Tip Units

The star blocks in this little miniature quilt are another example of quilt blocks made from the versatile half-square triangle unit. Because the patches are small, we'll assemble the units using a slightly different technique than we used in other chapters so that you don't need to handle tiny squares.

Here is how to make the star tip units:

1. Use your rotary ruler to measure and mark vertical lines on the reverse side of the 1⅝" x 36" light fabric strip. The lines should be 1⅝" apart to create a series of squares that size along its length. Create twenty squares.
2. Align a 45-degree line on a square or long ruler with the top or bottom edge of the strip and draw a diagonal line to connect the first two vertical lines.
3. Repeat to connect the next two squares, but draw the line along the opposite angle.

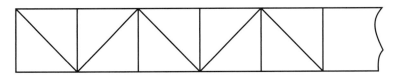

Fig. 10-2 **Drawing diagonal lines on grid**

4. Continue to mark the strip until all of the squares are connected by diagonal lines.

ELSEWHERE ON THE WEB

▶ Mosaic Quilt Studio offers a software program that helps you enlarge and print a photo in small fabric squares to create a mosaic quilt of the image. You can use photos of all types, but you'll love the results from close-up images of people—they are so realistic. You can manipulate the images in lots of ways to enhance them or create special effects. Pay a visit to the company's Web site the next time you are on the Internet at www.mosaicquilt.com.

▶ Thangles are preprinted fabric strips that make it easy to sew half-square triangles. Cut strips of fabric and pin them to Thangles. Sew on the lines and follow the directions in the packet to finish the units. Use the Thangles Mini Pack to make the ¾" finished-size units for the miniature version of this quilt. Use the 1½" finished-size Thangles for the larger version of the quilt near the end of this chapter. Visit www.thangles.com.

5. If you do not have a quarter-inch presser foot, use your ruler to draw lines that are a scant ¼" from each side of the original angled lines.

6. Align the 1⅝" x 36" dark star tip fabric with the marked strip, right sides together and edges matched exactly. Use several straight pins to hold the two strips together.

7. Begin sewing at one end of the strip. Sew on the second set of marked lines or use your quarter-inch foot to sew scant ¼" seams along one side of the original diagonal lines. Stop sewing and pivot at the end of each line in order to continue along the length of the strip.

8. Remove the strip from the sewing machine and sew additional seams on the opposite side of the original diagonal lines.

9. Use your rotary cutter and ruler to cut the strip apart on vertical lines. Use sharp scissors instead if you find that method is an easier way to cut small patches.

10. Cut again on the diagonal line between the two seam lines on each square unit. You should now have forty half-square triangle units.

11. Put the units on your ironing board, dark triangle up. Place a warm iron on top of each unit to set its seam. Press each unit open and trim off triangular nubs that extend past seam allowances.

12. Each half-square triangle unit should measure 1¼" square.

Assemble the Star Quilt

1. Cut twenty 1½" squares from the 1¼" x 26" light background fabric strips.

2. Choose four 1½" background squares, eight half-square triangle units, and one 2" center square. Arrange the components into three rows.

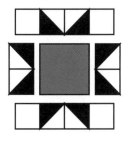

Fig. 10-3 **Arrange star block components**

3. Sew the components of each row together. Press seam allowances away from half-square triangle units when possible.
4. Sew the three rows together to complete the block, matching seams carefully. Press.
5. Repeat to make a total of four star blocks.
6. Make the center block with remaining block components. Arrange the eight half-square triangle units to form one point that radiates outward from each side of the block's center square. Sew the rows together. The block is similar to a traditional block called Square-in-a-Square.

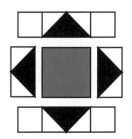

Fig. 10-4 **Arrange center block components**

Sew the quilt blocks and alternate blocks into rows. Now it's time to arrange the blocks into rows. After we sew all the rows

ASK YOUR GUIDE

What is a miniature quilt? Does a quilt have to be tiny to be classified as a mini?

▶ A miniature is broadly defined as any object that's a reduced-scale version of the original. In quilting, we usually call any quilt with blocks that measure 4" square or under a miniature. If you're not comfortable working that small, start out with 5" or 6" blocks, working smaller as you become more familiar with quiltmaking.

together we'll add the borders, and when that's complete you'll be well on the way to finishing this little quilt. Refer to the quilt layout drawing at the beginning of this chapter for a visual look at quilt rows, and look at the quilt photo in the color insert.

Follow these steps to arrange the blocks into rows:

1. Arrange the top row by placing a 3½" alternate block between two star blocks.
2. Arrange the middle row by placing a 3½" alternate block on each side of the square-in-a-square block.
3. Repeat the arrangement of row 1 to make row 3.
4. Sew the components of each row together. Press seam allowances toward the alternate blocks.
5. Sew the rows together, matching seam intersections carefully. Press.

Add the inner and outer borders to the quilt. Refer to Chapter 4 for instructions that explain how to measure the quilt and sew butted borders to its sides. Use 1¼" wide strips of the light border fabric for the inner borders. Use 2¾" wide strips of paisley for the outer border.

Now it's time to finish the miniature quilt. Refer to the instructions in Chapter 9 to finish the miniature quilt. Use a low-loft batting so that the quilt will hang flat against a wall. I did simple straight-line machine quilting along patch edges, and then added small red hearts at the center of each alternate block.

Take one more step to add a hanging sleeve to your quilt. You can add a hanging sleeve to any quilt, but it's particularly important for miniatures and wall hangings that you plan to hang on a wall. A sleeve stretches the entire width of the back of

▶ Martingale & Company sells a Baby Bias Square Ruler that's perfect for making little triangle units and cutting small segments. It measures just 4" square and has very narrow lines that let you see exactly where you're positioning fabric for cutting—and that improves your accuracy. Visit http://store .martingale-pub.com and enter baby bias square ruler into the search window.

the quilt, making it easy to insert a dowel or curtain rod for display. Don't be tempted to hang a quilt on the wall by tacking it up with straight pins along its edges, because that method will eventually distort the quilt and cause it to sag at unsupported locations.

You can add a hanging sleeve before or after the quilt is bound. Using this easy method, the height of the sleeve conforms to the rules of many quilt shows. If it's deeper than you require for home display, cut strips that are somewhat narrower.

WHAT'S HOT

▶ You can add hanging sleeve to the quilt when you sew on the binding, sewing its length all the way across the top of the quilt with strong machine stitching. That method creates a bit of bulk within binding, but it provides an extra strong sleeve for heavy quilts. You'll find the instructions on my About.com Quilting Web site at http://about.com/quilt ing/hangingsleeve.

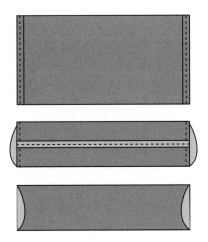

Fig. 10-5 **Make a hanging sleeve**

Follow these steps to add a hanging sleeve:

1. Cut or piece together a fabric strip that's 9" tall and the same width as your quilt.
2. Fold under the short edges ¼", placing wrong sides together. Fold again and press.
3. Sew a straight seam to hem the folds.
4. Fold the strip lengthwise, wrong sides together and aligning raw edges. Sew the raw edges together with a ½" seam allowance. Press the seam allowance open.

ELSEWHERE ON THE WEB

▶ Robinson's Wood Crafts is one company that makes wooden hangers for your quilts. You'll find quilt hangers that let you drape a quilt over a dowel and hangers that grasp the quilt all the way along its top edge. Robinson's also carries wrought iron hangers and traditional wooden quilt racks at www .robinsonswoodcrafts.com.

5. Center the tube on the quilt backing with the pressed open seam against the backing and the top edge of the tube about ½" below the binding.
6. Hand stitch the top edge of the tube to the quilt backing. Stitch into the batting occasionally to help strengthen the seam.
7. Smooth the sleeve downward along the back of the quilt. Make a ½" fold near its bottom edge to create a pleat. Leaving the pleat intact, pin the bottom of the sleeve to the quilt.
8. Hand stitch the lower edge of the sleeve to the quilt. Remove the pins.
9. Hand stitch the back edges of the sleeve to the quilt. Leave the front edges unsewn to allow for rod insertion.

Make a Larger Star Quilt

A slightly larger version of this quilt would make a nice wall hanging or cover for a small table. Assemble the components exactly as you would for the smaller quilt. You'll need extra yardage to cut larger pieces of fabric. The larger quilt has 6" blocks and finishes at 31" x 31", exactly double the size of the miniature. The increased size allows you to showcase fabrics that are printed with a slightly larger print scale.

If you like retro fabrics, I think the larger quilt would look nice sewn with some of the juvenile prints that are available. They depict children from past eras running and playing and having a good time. Fabric lines usually include a larger pictorial that would be perfect for the squares, and smaller-scale prints that could be used in other areas. Some of the fabric lines are available as traditional quilting cottons and in flannel.

The following tables explain fabric and yardage requirements, as well as cutting guidelines for the larger star quilt. After gathering your fabric, simply follow the assembly steps above for the mini quilt to create a larger star quilt.

FABRIC REQUIREMENTS

Fabric	Yardage
Paisley	⅝ yard
Light, inner border	⅓ yard
Light, star backgrounds	⅜ yard
Dark, star tips and binding	¾ yard
Pictorial, star centers	⅛ yard

CUTTING CHART

Fabric Required	Patch Size	Number Required
Paisley	6½" x 27" strip	1
	reserve remainder for border, cut 4" strips	
Light, inner border	cut 2" strips after assembly	
Light, star backgrounds	2" x 42" strip	1
	2⅜" x 42" strip	2
Dark, star tips	2⅜" x 42" strip	2
	reserve remainder for binding	
Pictorial	3½" x 3½" squares	5

WHAT'S HOT

▶ Fabrics that feature animals would also be another good match for this quilt. There are lots of choices that have panels full of blocklike squares to sew at the star centers. You'll find fabrics that feature just about any animal you want to honor in a quilt, both domestic and wild. Laurel Burch is famous for her animal prints, but you'll find many other prints with animal motifs from a variety of textile designers.

Making a Dollhouse Miniature Quilt

Dollhouse minis are made to an even smaller scale than typical miniature quilts. The most popular miniature size is based on a 12:1 ratio. In other words, every twelve inches of an object's original size is reduced to one inch in the miniature version. That means a 12" square block would be reduced to 1", and a 15" square block would equal 1¼". Multiply the original finished size of a quilt block by 0.083 and round up to the nearest ⅛" to figure other sizes.

The reduction sounds difficult, but it can be easily accomplished with a few simple techniques. One way is to find a pictorial fabric with small motifs. Cut 1½" or larger squares, placing the design you wish to feature in the center of the square. Cut plain sashing strips ⅝" wide and in a length that matches the block width. After sewing they'll finish at ⅛". Be sure you're sewing an exact ¼" seam allowance before you begin—even a small inaccuracy will be noticeable in such a small quilt. Refer to Chapter 4 for more information about sashing. You'll find seam allowance guidelines in Chapter 7.

Foundation piecing is another excellent choice for dollhouse miniatures. That technique makes it easy to sew perfect mini blocks—even if they contain lots of pieces. If you can sew a straight seam on a line, you can make a foundation-pieced quilt, no matter how small it is. Be sure to read Chapter 8 to learn more about foundation piecing. You can reduce the Courthouse Steps block in Appendix C to a small mini size, and then add a ¼" seam allowance around its edges to create a miniature template. Refer to the assembly instructions in Chapter 8 to construct the block, but use strips of fabric that are about ½" wider than the "logs" in the block. Trim seams back to about ⅛" as you sew.

Here are a few layout options for dollhouse miniature quilts. Dollhouse minis sometimes fit little beds more neatly when the two corner blocks in the bottom row are omitted. The little gap on each side lets you tuck the bottom of the quilt between the mattress and footboard, while allowing the sides of the quilt to fall along the mattress.

Don't let your dollhouse mini look like a potholder! It's usually best not to add batting to dollhouse miniature quilts, especially if they have lots of closely spaced seams that add bulk to the quilt top. Too much loft makes quilts stiff and difficult to drape on little beds. If you must add a bit of depth, use silk batting or peel a thin layer away from a piece of regular cotton batting—just enough to add a bit of loft.

If sides don't drape nicely, use one of these techniques to coax them in place:

- If you used color-stable, prewashed fabrics to make the quilt, dampen the top of the quilt slightly and mold it in place on the bed. Use a bit of spray starch to help form the shape if necessary, and then allow the quilt to dry in an airy location.
- Insert a length of fine wire along the edges of the quilt and bend the wire to give the sides of the quilt a draped appearance. You can also use polyester boning, which is sold in fabric shops.

Use a single layer of binding to finish these little quilts, because double-fold binding usually adds too much bulk around outer edges. Sew the binding in place with an $\frac{1}{8}$" seam allowance, using the instructions in Chapter 9 as a guide.

WHAT'S HOT

▶ Use a $\frac{1}{4}$" seam allowance to sew dollhouse miniatures, but trim each seam back to about $\frac{1}{8}$" to reduce bulk. That's a lot easier than setting up your sewing machine to sew a $\frac{1}{8}$" seam and then changing pattern instructions to compensate for the difference. Be especially careful to trim seam allowances in foundation-pieced minis, which typically have more overlapped fabric on their reverse sides.

Quick and Easy Fabric Postcards

Fabric postcards are another fun quilting project that we can slot into the miniature quilt category simply because they finish at 4" x 6". Postcards needn't be intricately pieced—you can use any technique you like to make them. A method you've never used is postcard perfect—if you make a mistake or don't enjoy the process you can move on to another idea without worrying that you've wasted lots of time and materials.

You're probably wondering if fabric postcards can be mailed. Yes they can, and what a nice way to send someone a truly personal card for any occasion. You can construct and embellish the cards any way you like, but there are some things you can do to make sure they arrive at their destination in good shape.

Your finished postcard should measure no more than 4" x 6" and be ⅛" or less thick in order to mail it at the regular postcard rate. You can mail larger or thicker cards, but you will pay additional postage for them. Most quilters use a slightly larger base to build their postcards, and then trim them back to the correct size after the design is complete. Just be sure not to add design elements in an area that will be trimmed away. Mailing and return addresses can be on the front or back of your card—just like paper postcards.

Fabric postcards have three layers. The top and backing are fabric, and the inner batting is usually created by fusing an interfacing between the other layers. Timtex is a stiff interfacing that works nicely for postcards. It does not contain fusible web, so you'll need to add that to your postcard front and back, then press onto the Timtex. The thin version of fast2fuse is a similar product that already contains fusible web. Both are available from companies that specialize in quilting merchandise.

Embellish either side of your postcard in any way you desire—keeping in mind the ⅛" thickness limit.

- Fuse appliqué shapes onto the fabric.
- Sew small beads onto the card.
- Use machine embroidery or decorative machine stitches.
- Stitch through tulle or netting to hold down yarns and other fibers.
- Zigzag stitch over yarns and laces.

There's no limit to the types of adornments you can add to your fabric postcards.

Postcards with mailing and return addresses on their backs needn't be plain. Add embellishments if you like, but make sure the addresses are readable. You can hand-write addresses with a permanent marker, or you can print them on fabric, apply fusible web, and press them to your postcard. Place a bit of decorative stitching around them to camouflage the fused lines. Postcards are also a wonderful place to use all sorts of decorative threads. Mix colors and types of threads as much as you like.

You'll find a few postcard back designs in Appendix C. Scan each design into your computer at 100 percent and print on cloth. The design should measure 4" x 6". Cut out on the lines and use for the backs of your postcards.

When your postcard fronts and backs are complete, fuse the stiff interfacing between them. The easiest way to finish the edges is with decorative stitches. Satin stitching is one choice, but any type of stitches will work just fine. If your sewing machine can't sew fancy stitches, try sewing three parallel lines of straight stitches around the edges of the card. Use variegated thread or three different colors of thread to add a bit of variety.

Print photos and designs on your inkjet or laser printer. Photos of friends, family, favorite places, and events add a truly personal touch to your fabric postcards. Download photos from your digital camera or use a scanner to put images on your computer.

I use Bubble Jet Set 2000 to prepare my fabric before printing on an inkjet printer. Follow the instructions on the bottle, and the designs you print will be permanent. The company makes another product, Bubble Jet Rinse, which is used to remove excess inks and Bubble Jet Set after printing. You do not need to pretreat fabrics that will be printed on a laser printer.

I like to use white fabric when I want photos to be very visible. Cut the fabric slightly larger than necessary and use a hot iron to press it onto the shiny side of freezer paper. Cut it back to the exact size required—any size that you can feed through your printer. This method ensures that the fabric is adhered to the paper all the way around its edges. Freezer-backed paper works equally well in laser and inkjet printers.

You can save a step later by pressing Pellon Wonder-Under to the reverse side of paper before printing it on an inkjet printer. Stick with freezer paper for inkjet printing.

You might need to experiment a bit before your prints look just the way you want them to look, because identical photos are often more pale when printed on fabric than they are when printed on paper. Sometimes it's helpful to use your photo preparation software to increase the color saturation. You'll find lots of photo printing tips and techniques on the About.com Quilting Web site.

To make laser prints permanent, spray on three or four thin coats of Krylon Workable Fixatiff, available from art suppliers. Use the spray in a well-ventilated area and be sure to let the fabric dry between coats.

The last thing to do is put a self-adhesive stamp on your postcard and drop it in the mail!

Get Linked

Do you like making miniature quilts? They're among my favorites because I enjoy working in the reduced scale. Stop by the About.com Quilting site when you're looking for miniature quilt patterns and other resources.

WALK AROUND THE BLOCK QUILT

This strip-pieced miniature quilt is very easy to make. It features a center medallion that's surrounded by a series of nine-patch and bar units.

http://about.com/quilting/walkaroundtheblock

MOTHER'S FANTASY WINDOWS

A miniature quilt made with Attic Windows blocks, but with a twist. Instead of same-sized blocks placed side by side, this quilt has a series of mix-and-match block variations.

http://about.com/quilting/atticwindows

Chapter 11

String-Pieced Table Runner

Learn the Freehand-Piecing Technique

You'll love how easily this table runner goes together. You can sew the runner quickly—and without any of the usual fuss about making sure patches are cut perfectly. Most of the assembly steps don't even require that you sew exact quarter-inch seams! Get ready to have fun learning a carefree technique that was invented by innovative—and thrifty—quilters.

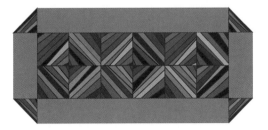

Fig. 11-1 String-pieced table runner

▶ Fat quarters are quarter yards of fabric that are configured differently than standard quarter-yard cuts. A standard cut measures about 9" x 44" and works well for strip piecing, which is accomplished with long, narrow strips of fabric. Standard cuts aren't as versatile for other tasks. That's where the fat quarter steps in, created by cutting a yard into four large chunks that each measure 18" x 22". Fat eighths are similar, but measure 9" x 22".

We'll use a method called string piecing to assemble the table runner. It's a type of foundation piecing, which you read about in Chapter 8, but with foundation templates that are a bit different—they aren't marked with a pattern. Long strips of fabric—the strings—are sewn freehand onto oversized muslin squares, which are trimmed back to the perfect size after assembly. Easy pieced triangles repeat the string look at the corners of the table runner.

String piecing is known as a "make do" form of quilting, a method that lets quilters use up every bit of fabric scraps in their stash. Although we purchase most of our fabrics specifically for quilting now, including fabrics for our string projects, past generations of quilters discovered that string piecing was an excellent way to use up leftover fabrics from sewing garments. The method also helped quilters recycle fabrics cut from worn-out clothing.

We'll use muslin as a foundation for our string-pieced quilts. Past quilters sometimes used leftover fabrics and worn textiles for that component, too. Traditional foundations were sometimes made from paper, which was removed after the blocks were sewn together. The outer edges of my table runner are made from a colorful border print filled with butterflies.

Get started by choosing a border print with several sets of repeating borders printed across its width. A border between 3" and 5" wide works nicely for the table runner. And although a border print is perfect for this layout, it's not a requirement. Use any combination of fabrics that suits your style.

Get ready to string piece the quilt blocks. The table runner's blocks each measure 8" square after they're sewn together, making the size of the strip-pieced interior 16" x 48". If you need a longer table runner, an additional group of four blocks will increase the length by 16". The overall size of the runner depends on the fabric you use in the border.

FABRIC REQUIREMENTS

Fabric	Yardage
Muslin	1¼ yard
Border print	1¾ yard
Nine assorted fabrics, light to dark	⅓ yard each
Backing	1¾ yard
Flannel	1¾ yard
Binding	⅓ yard

CUTTING CHART

Fabric	Patch Size	Number Required
Muslin	9" x 42" strips	3
Assorted	long strips, 1½" to 2½" wide	Number varies

Assemble the String-Pieced Blocks

Muslin often shrinks quite a bit when it's washed and dried. Using it straight off the bolt, and combining it with fabrics that shrink only a little, can cause puckering and distortion the first time your quilted items are laundered. Prewash all of your fabrics before you cut strips from them.

Here is how to assemble the string-pieced blocks:

1. Use your rotary cutting equipment to cut twelve 9" x 9" muslin squares from your 9" x 42" muslin strips.

TOOLS YOU NEED

▶ Choose a light to medium gray thread to piece your blocks. It will blend with many different colors and shades of printed fabrics. Set up an iron and ironing board near your sewing machine. Make sure your rotary blade is in good shape before you begin cutting and that your long ruler and square ruler are near your cutting mat. You'll sew through lots of layers, so insert a new all-purpose needle in your sewing machine.

Fig. 11-2 **Making a string-pieced block**

2. Place a long string right-side up on top of a square, from one corner to an opposite corner. The beginning end of the strip should extend just past the muslin corner. Trim the long tail so that it extends just past the square at the opposite corner. Just cut it off straight—there's no need to trim its edges at angles.

3. Place another strip of fabric right-side down along the first, matching long edges on one side. Do not trim it back yet, but make sure its ends both extend past the muslin square.

4. Do a little experiment to make sure the ends will be long enough to cover the muslin square when the new piece is flipped right-side up. Pin the strip in place along what will be its seam line—¼" from the aligned edges. Fold the strip right-side up and inspect its outer edges. They should still overlap the muslin square. If they don't, reposition the strip and check again. You'll only need to do this a few times, because you'll quickly develop a feel for the amount of overlap that's required for each string.

5. Remove the pins and sew a seam approximately ¼" from the aligned edge. The seam doesn't have to be exactly ¼", but it should be straight. Remove from the machine and flip the new strip right-side up. Trim the excess string tail if necessary.

6. Align a second string along the opposite long edge of the first string, right-side down. Check placement, then sew along the matched edges. Remove from the machine.

7. Flip the piece right-side up and trim the excess string tail.

8. Take the block to the ironing board and press both new pieces in place.
9. Use the same method to add two more strings, first on one side of the group and then the other. Flip the new strings right-side up, trim back tails as needed, then press both in place. Continue adding strings, two at a time, until the entire muslin square is covered.
10. Take the block to your rotary cutting mat. Use a large, square ruler to cut it exactly 8½" square. Repeat to make a total of eleven string pieced blocks.

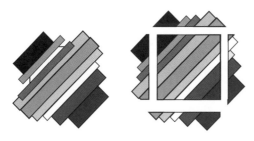

Fig. 11-3 Trim block to 8½" square

Use chain piecing to speed up assembly. Your blocks will go together even faster if you chain piece them. Place the first string on a muslin square and sew the second string to it. Don't remove the foundation from the sewing machine—just keep sewing until it's no longer under the needle.

Sew the first two strings to the next square and let the square move beyond the needle. Continue sewing until all of the squares have the first two strings attached. Snip the threads between the squares and begin sewing again, adding the third string to the opposite side of the middle string of all blocks. Snip the threads and press strips right-side up. Continue sewing two strings at a time to all blocks until the entire square is covered.

ASK YOUR GUIDE

Why do I need a square ruler?

▶ A square ruler is important for many quilting tasks because it helps you check the size of quilt blocks and other components. Put any block under the ruler and its marked lines show you immediately if any part of the block is off size. I have several square rulers and tend to grab the smallest one that will do the job. Start with a 15½" square ruler and add to your collection over time.

Chain piecing is like sewing on an assembly line. It reduces the amount of thread you use and cuts down on the number of trips you make to the ironing board.

Use these string-piecing tips to make the quilt blocks. String piecing is easy and almost effortless, but there are a few things you can do to make sure your finished blocks are sewn just right. We've already taken one precaution by using oversize muslin squares and trimming them back after sewing, because string foundations often shrink a bit in size and become distorted during assembly. Here are a few more techniques that will help you make accurate and attractive string blocks.

▶ To cut threads from chain piecing more efficiently, insert a seam ripper with a round, penlike handle into the hole on a spool of thread—handle down. Hold a chain-pieced unit in each hand and slip the threads that separate them down onto the ripper's cutting end, which is standing straight up at the center of the spool. Be sure to avoid injuring yourself by removing the seam ripper from the spool when you're not using it to cut threads.

- Use your wider strips at the corners of muslin squares so that corner patches don't become too small when the squares are trimmed back.
- I used dark strings at the outer corners of my blocks because I like the emphasis they provide when the blocks are sewn together. You might prefer lights in the corners, a specific color, or a totally random arrangement.
- Don't worry about positioning your fabrics to match or placing darks next to lights. The blocks will be charming no matter how you arrange your fabrics. Just grab a strip and sew!
- Sometimes it's difficult to determine where the muslin foundation is when it's time to square up the blocks. Flip them over and make the first two cuts with the reverse side facing up.

Design the Table Runner

It's time to arrange the string blocks side by side. The layout drawing at the beginning of this chapter shows one option for placement. Start there by using these instructions, but don't hesitate to arrange the blocks in a completely different way. The string-pieced blocks will look very different if you vary their positions, so flip them around a bit to see if you prefer another layout. The choice is yours.

Follow these steps to design your ideal table runner:

1. Referring to the table runner layout drawing in Figure 11-1, arrange the blocks on a design wall, placing them into two rows of six blocks.
2. Step back and look at the arrangement. Do you like how the strips come together? Would the piece look more color balanced if you rearranged the blocks? Give that a try and inspect the runner again. Keep rearranging until you're happy with the layout.
3. Leave the room for awhile and return. Do you still like the arrangement? Once you're sure it suits you, sew the blocks together into horizontal rows. Press the seams in each row in opposite directions. Match adjoining seams carefully and sew the rows together. Press the new seam open or to one side.

Add the Borders and Finish the Runner

Read all instructions before cutting borders for your quilt. Use the method described in Chapter 4 to measure the vertical and horizontal dimensions of the table runner. You'll need two borders to match each length—but add ½" to each to allow for corner-block seam allowances.

If you're using a border print, the print on your fabric will determine border width. A stripe with a finished width between 3" to 4" will work just fine.

How can I make a string-pieced border?

▶ It's easy to make a string-pieced border for your quilt. Cut border strips that are slightly longer and wider than the unfinished size of your border. Sew strings to them just as you did the blocks, placing the strings across the short width of the strip. When you're finished, square up the strip and sew it to the quilt. Since this quilt has a string-pieced center, I suggest that you separate the outer border from the central runner by adding a narrow border cut from a single fabric. The narrow border helps tone down the busy design of the strings.

Use any print fabric for the borders if you do not have a border print. Cut 4" wide strips along the fabric's lengthwise grain to make borders, or piece them from crosswise-grain strips.

Here is how to add the border onto your quilt:

1. Use rotary equipment to cut a border stripe from the entire length of your fabric, aligning your rotary ruler to leave a ¼" seam allowance along each long edge. Many border prints have printed lines along their outer edges that make handy seam guides. If yours has a line, be sure to cut ¼" past it.
2. Add ½" to the short (side) border length determined when you measured the table runner. Divide that number by two.
3. For symmetry along the sides of the table runner, choose a specific place in the border print to use as the midpoint for all of your borders and mark the spot. We'll measure outwards from that portion of the motif to cut each border.
4. Beginning at the mark, measure outwards in each direction, ending on each side at the distance calculated in step 2. Mark the end points—they should be mirror images of each other.
5. Place the border along one short side of the runner, with its midpoint matched to the midpoint of the table runner's side. The border's marked endpoints should extend ¼" past the ends of the runner. Cut the border straight across at each end mark.
6. Place the cut strip on top of the remaining long strip, aligning the motifs so that both layers are identical. Cut the bottom strip to match the length of the top strip.
7. Fold a side border strip in half crosswise and finger crease. Place it right-side down along one side of the runner, matching

the crease with the runner's center seam. Align the remaining edges with the runner. Sew the border to the runner with a ¼" seam, using the border stripe's printed line as a guide if possible. Press the seam allowance toward the border.

8. Repeat to add a border to the opposite side of the runner.

Make the corner triangles and the long border. Before you sew the long borders to the table runner you'll sew string-pieced triangles to their ends. If you prefer, use the instructions to sew a square at the ends of borders instead of a triangle.

Here is how to make corner triangles or squares and the long border:

1. To make corner triangles, cut two muslin squares with sides that are 2" longer than the finished width of your border (cut width minus ½"). For instance, if the border finishes at 4" wide, cut two 6" squares.

2. To make corner squares instead of triangles, cut four muslin squares with sides that are ¾" longer than the finished width of your border.

3. String piece the small squares just as you did the larger squares, starting with a wide fabric strip placed on the center diagonal.

4. If you're making triangles, cut each square in half from one corner to the other along the lengthwise center of that wider fabric strip. Use your rotary cutting equipment to trim the triangle so that it's short sides are ⅞" longer than the finished width of the border.

5. If you're making squares, trim them to measure the cut width of your border stripe.

ELSEWHERE ON THE WEB

▶ I love the border-print feedsacks that were made during the first half of the twentieth century. Home-makers bought grain, flour, sugar, and lots of other staples in cloth bags that could be recycled for clothing, aprons, dish towels—and quilts. Border prints were perfect for making thrifty pillowcases. You can see and buy a wide variety of colorful, vintage border-print feedsacks at Sharon's Antiques and Vintage Fabrics, www.rickrack.com/bordsk.html.

WHAT'S HOT

▶ Prairie points are small folded triangles that are created from squares of fabric. They are most often used to finish the edges of a quilt. You'll find step-by-step instructions for two different types of prairie points on the About.com Quilting Web site at http://about.com/quilting/prairiepoints.

6. Cut two long border strips for the quilt using the same method you used to cut the side strips. Use the same midpoint for the long borders.
7. Sew a corner triangle to each end of a long border strip as shown in the table runner layout, Figure 11-1. Press seam allowances toward the border strips.
8. Sew the border strips to the quilt, matching edges carefully. Press seam allowances toward the border strip.

It's time to finish the table runner. Refer to the instructions in Chapter 9 to finish the table runner. The string-pieced section of the table runner is made from three layers of fabric, so it's naturally thicker than the single-fabric borders. Add a little depth under the entire runner with a piece of low-loft cotton batting between the top and backing. Another batting alternative is flannel, which isn't quite as thick but will add stability.

The string-pieced center doesn't need to be heavily quilted— but use some simple machine stitches along seams to hold the layers firmly in place. Quilt as desired in the border. One option is to follow the lines of your border print.

Finish the table runner by sewing a mitered binding to the quilt's edges with a quarter-inch seam. Crossgrain strips should flow easily around angled triangle corners.

There are more ways to finish the outer edges of the quilt. It's best to finish bed quilts with durable bound edges, but small quilted projects like this table runner can be completed using other techniques. One method is called knife edges. Another is known by several names, but it is often called self binding.

Follow these steps for knife-edge binding:

1. Square up the quilted runner. Move the quilt top and backing out of the way and trim ¼" off the batting along each side.
2. Turn under the quilt top by ¼" and press. Turn under the backing by ¼" and press. Tuck the batting into the fold of the backing. Work with the corners to fold them under neatly.
3. Baste the edges in place, matching folds carefully.
4. Use a straight machine stitch and matching thread to sew a straight stitch all the way around the quilt, about ⅛" from the outer edges.
5. To stabilize the edges, machine sew a line of quilting stitches about ¼" inward from each side of the quilt.

A self-edge binding is accomplished by bringing the backing fabric forward over the quilt top, turning it under, and then sewing it to the quilt.

Follow these steps for a self-edge binding:

1. Choose a backing fabric that coordinates with the quilt top and use it to sandwich the quilt. Be sure to make the backing large enough to fold over the quilt top when quilting is complete. Cutting it 3" wider and longer than your quilt top should allow plenty of extra fabric.
2. Quilt the top as desired. Move the backing out of the way and square up the quilt top and batting if necessary, making them the same size.
3. Trim the batting, leaving an excess that extends past the two top layers that's a little more than twice the width of your desired binding.
4. Fold a corner of the backing across a corner of the quilt top, forming a right triangle.

ELSEWHERE ON THE WEB

▶ Pathways into Quilt History is a Web site by Kimberley Wulfert. It offers several informative articles about dating vintage quilts. One article I found to be very interesting shows a gallery of vintage fabrics that were included in a salesman's sample book from 1939. It provides an excellent look at the types of fabrics string quilts were made from during the 1930s and 1940s. Visit www.antiquequiltdating.com/NYWorldsFairsamples.html.

▶ In this book I explain three methods that are used to finish the edges of a quilt, but there are additional techniques that you might want to try. You can sew long binding strips to each side of the quilt independently instead of applying a continuous binding with mitered edges. You might also choose to use a facing around the edges of the quilt in much the same way as a facing is applied to garments. Refer to the About.com Quilting Web site to learn more about these binding alternatives at http://about.com/quilting/binding.

5. Trim away the excess backing that extends past the fold. Make the cut across the tip of the fold, removing the triangular shape. The edge of the newly cut piece should meet the spots on each corner of the quilt where the two other layers of the quilt end.
6. Pin in place and repeat to prepare the remaining corners.
7. Fold the backing toward the front of the quilt along one side; the self binding should create a mitered edge along the folded corner. Pin in place.
8. Repeat, folding the binding along each side to create miters at each corner.
9. Sew the binding in place. Use a straight stitch and matching thread if you sew by machine. Use a blind stitch and matching thread if you prefer to sew by hand. Take a few stitches to secure miters and complete the quilt.

String-Quilt Variations

You're not limited to covering squares with long strings of fabric when you make a string-pieced quilt. You'll find a few string variations in Chapter 8, but there's really no end to the block variations you can create.

- Cut all strips into wedgelike shapes instead of using straight-sided strips. The angled strips will create a sunburst effect when sewn to the foundation.
- Don't sew long strings across the entire block. Try sewing shorter strips along the block's diagonal. When you've covered the central area, from corner to corner, begin sewing long strips placed perpendicular to the first, working on both sides until you've covered the opposite corners of the block.

- Sew strings lengthwise to a long strip of fabric. Square up the fabric and use it to cut triangles, squares, rectangles, diamonds, and other shapes. You'll find shape-cutting instructions in Chapter 6.
- Sew strings to rectangular foundations and cut them apart to produce long triangles. Sew mismatched triangles together to create scrappy rectangular blocks. Be sure to allow extra width and length for squaring up and seam allowances.
- Sew strings to a large foundation and use the new "fabric" to cut out shapes for appliqué.
- Experiment with your own designs, combining string blocks in different ways to create a unique layout.

Get Linked

Here are some places you might want to visit on my Quilting Web site on About.com. They offer inspiration and instructions to help you make a string-pieced quilt.

SAM'S SCRAPPY STRING QUILT

Take a look at this pretty string quilt, made by a member of our online quilting community for a little boy named Sam.
http://about.com/quilting/samsquilt

MAKE A STRING-PIECED DOG BANDANA

This string-pieced dog bandana goes together in a flash. It has rag edges between the patches and is very easy to customize for your special friend.
http://about.com/quilting/dogbandana

Chapter 12

Quick and Easy Rag Quilt

Rag Quilt Introduction

Get ready for a completely different type of quiltmaking experience, one where seam allowances become an important design element instead of being pressed to the side and tucked out of sight behind our quilt blocks. When we make a rag quilt, seam allowances are brought to the front of the quilt, where they flow together to create soft, chenillelike edges after the quilt is washed. You'll find a photograph of rag quilts made using this pattern in the color insert.

About

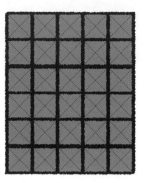

Fig. 12-1 **Rag quilt layout**

Most traditional quilts are created by assembling an entire quilt top, and then sandwiching the top with batting and backing. Next, the quilt is quilted. Finally, binding is sewn around its outer edges. You can forget about that progression of steps for a rag quilt, because the assembly process is quite a bit different.

Each block in the rag quilt is sandwiched with a same-sized square of batting and backing. The individual quilt sandwiches are sewn together to create rows, and when the rows are joined the quilt is nearly complete. There's no binding to deal with, and the only quilting is an optional X placed in each quilt sandwich.

Making a rag quilt does require us to change a few sewing habits. We're accustomed to sewing our patches right sides together so that the seam allowance ends up behind our quilt blocks. But we want the seam allowance to be visible on the front of our rag quilts. In order to do that all units are sewn with backing sides together. That sounds simple, but if you're accustomed to sewing the traditional way it's a little hard to get used to.

You'll sew the blocks together with a ½" seam allowance—another change from traditional quiltmaking. The throat plate of your sewing machine probably has a groove that's ½" from the needle. Put a bit of masking tape along that line to help you remember that you're sewing a wider than normal seam.

If you have a walking foot, put it on your sewing machine. The foot's built-in feed dogs will work in sync with the machine's feed dogs to keep your components flowing through the machine smoothly.

Let's decide which fabrics to use. Flannel and homespun fabrics are two excellent choices for rag quilts. Both are slightly thicker than quilting cottons—they're soft and their raw edges fray nicely. Feel free to use regular quilting cottons if you prefer, because their edges fray just fine. Lightweight denim fabrics are a good choice when you want to make a heavier rag quilt. Avoid bluejean-weight denims unless you want a quilt that's super heavy.

The lap quilt that I'll walk you through in the steps below has a flannel batting. Save your more expensive flannel for the block fronts and choose any plain or printed flannel for the batting—you can even make use of flannel scraps from previous projects. The frayed edges of your batting and backing will be visible along rag seams, so avoid colors you don't feel will enhance the block fabrics.

Repeat flannels or homespun fabrics in the backing, or choose one or more traditional quilting cottons. This rag quilt is reversible, so having a nice assortment of fabrics on the back means it will look great no matter how it's laying. My rag quilt is made with flannels on the front and cotton fabrics on the back. You'll find a photograph of it in the color insert.

It's easy to add frayed-edge appliqué to your quilt blocks. Appliqué shapes can be added to all or just a portion of your rag quilt. Choose simple shapes with continuous outlines, like large flowers with gentle outer edges—shapes that are recognizable

ASK YOUR GUIDE

What are homespun fabrics?

▶ The motifs we see on typical quilting cottons are designs printed on the surface of plain white or colored cloth. Homespuns are made by weaving the fabric with different colors of thread. The design you see is actually a part of each fabric's structure. Most quilt shops and other fabric stores stock at least a few homespun fabrics, usually stripes and plaids. Homespuns are also called yarn-dyed fabrics, so be sure to search for that term when you look for homespun fabrics online.

without requiring a lot of detail. You can even stack shapes by using two images, identical or different, one on top of the other. Make sure to leave enough space around each shape to allow for a seam allowance.

Gingerbread men would look nice on a holiday-themed rag quilt. Stars with slightly rounded tips would fray nicely. Hearts are another good choice, and they can be identical or cut whimsically in lots of different styles. You can even cut out designs from a printed fabric, leaving a ¼"–½" seam allowance around the shape. That method is a quick and easy way to add color and interest to your rag quilt. You'll find a selection of simple appliqué shapes in Appendix C.

Make rigid templates of the appliqué shapes you would like to use. Trace around the shapes on the front side of fabric, leaving an inch or so between each tracing. Cut out the shapes ¼"–½" from the marked line.

Arrange the appliqué shapes on the block sandwiches before you sew rows together. It's a good idea to preview your block and appliqué on a design wall before you begin sewing. When you're satisfied with the layout, sew each appliqué shape to its block sandwich along the shape's original marked line. Use scissors to clip straight into the seam allowance about every ¼", taking care not to cut seams.

There's no need to stitch an X in blocks with appliqué. If shapes are large, consider quilting within them to help keep their interiors flush against the block fabrics. Follow the remaining instructions to finish your rag quilt.

FINISHED QUILT AND BLOCK SIZES

Finished Block Size	Finished Quilt Size
9" x 9"	45½" x 54½"

Choose a thread that blends or contrasts with your fabrics. Gather your long straight pins and set up an iron and ironing board. Insert a sharp rotary blade and make sure your long ruler and 12½" square ruler are nearby. You'll sew through lots of layers, so insert a new, all-purpose needle in your sewing machine. Adjust the machine to sew short stitches, about twelve to fifteen per inch. Have a sharp pair of scissors handy. You'll find other tool suggestions throughout the chapter.

FABRIC REQUIREMENTS

Position	Fabric	Yardage
Block fronts	Assorted flannels	2½ yards
Backing	Flannel, homespun or cotton prints	2½ yards
Batting	Flannel	2½ yards

CUTTING CHART

Position	Patch Size	Number Required
Block fronts	10" x 10" square	30
Backing	10" x 10" square	30
Batting	10" x 10" square	30

Make the Quilt Sandwiches

Quilt-block fronts are sandwiched with pieces of batting and backing before sewing the first seam. Align edges carefully and pay close attention to each fabric's orientation, because assembling a rag quilt is slightly different than the method you use to assemble traditional quilt blocks.

Follow these steps to make quilt sandwiches for your rag quilt:

ELSEWHERE ON THE WEB

1. Make thirty quilt-block sandwiches from your backing, batting, and block fabrics. Begin by placing a 10" × 10" backing square right-side down on your work table. Center a square of flannel batting on top of it, then place a 10" square of block fabric right-side up on top of the batting. Make sure the edges of all squares are aligned. Secure the layers with a few straight pins.

▶ Some quilters like to use a basting spray to hold quilt layers in place. Spray a very thin mist onto each side of batting squares, then sandwich the batting between the quilt block and backing fabrics—there's no need for straight pins! Follow the manufacturer's instructions and be sure to work in a well-ventilated room. Use as little spray as possible to avoid excess residue that can gum up your sewing machine needles and other components. Sullivan's Quilt Basting Spray is one choice (www.sullivans.net/usa).

2. Continue stacking and pinning until all thirty sets are sandwiched.
3. Arrange the blocks side by side on a design wall or any flat surface, creating six rows with five squares in each row. Refer back to the quilt layout drawing, Figure 12-1, at the beginning of the chapter.
4. If you're making a scrappy quilt, step back and look at the layout. Are you happy with the design? If not, rearrange blocks until you like the effect. Leave the room for a few minutes then return—sometimes distancing ourselves from a design for awhile helps us recognize ways to improve it.

Sew the Quilt Blocks Together

These might be the easiest quilt blocks you'll ever sew. Three squares of fabric each, with a few seams to prequilt them—what could be simpler? The blocks move through your sewing machine quickly when you develop a routine to accomplish all steps in factory-line style.

Follow these steps to sew the rag-quilt blocks together:

1. Remove the blocks in the top row, row 1, stacking them near your sewing machine and keeping them in order.

2. Optional step: Stitch from one corner to the opposite corner in each to create a stitched X on the face of the block. Use matching or contrasting thread, depending on the look you want to achieve. If you're not comfortable stitching the X freehand, align your rotary ruler along each diagonal and mark the line lightly with a chalk pencil.

Finish Assembling the Quilt

The way you sew the blocks and rows together is another step that makes a rag quilt truly unique. You'll learn the technique very quickly and you'll be anxious to make another quilt because it's so fast and easy. Remember the phrase, align backings together for sewing, and you'll do just fine.

Follow these steps to finish assembling your rag quilt:

1. Sew the blocks in row 1 together along their sides, taking care to keep them in their original order. Use a ½" seam allowance and align blocks with backing sides together. Finger press seams open on the front of the quilt blocks.
2. Return row 1 to the design wall. Remove the blocks in row 2 from the wall and sew them together just as you did the blocks in row 1. Repeat for all six rows.
3. Sew the rows together with a ½" seam allowances, taking care to align backing edges together before sewing. Finger press long seams open on the front of the quilt.
4. Sew a ½" seam along each side of the quilt, extending seams to the ends of blocks.
5. Use a sharp pair of scissors to clip straight into seam allowances about every ¼", including allowances around the outer edges of the quilt. Be careful not to cut into the seam line.

▶ Hera markers are wonderful little tools that are used to mark lines on cloth. The best part is that lines aren't actually drawn at all, they're creases that disappear with handling or when the quilt is washed. That means there's no chance of having a permanent, unwanted marking on your quilt. You'll find Hera markers for sale at most local and online quilt shops.

There's no need to clip the raw edges of your appliqué shapes.

Fig. 12-2 **Clip seam allowances**

6. Wash the quilt in the washing machine. If you use soap at all, use a mild detergent or a soap made especially for quilts, such as Orvus Paste. Stop the machine during the wash and rinse cycle and inspect the water. There probably won't be too many loose threads, but if there are, remove any floating on top of the water to help avoid clogged drains when the tub empties.
7. When the wash cycle is complete, dry the quilt in the dryer. Clip off loose threads if necessary. If you want the quilt to be more ragged, wash it again.

That's it! The quilt is finished, and the exposed seams will become even more frayed with each wash. Turn the quilt over and you'll see that the seams on the back are hidden—just like the seams in a traditionally pieced quilt. The rag quilt looks fantastic no matter which way you display it.

Here are a few options for your next rag quilt. This little project might have been your first rag quilt, but I'll bet it won't be your last. Rag quilts are so quick and easy to put together that you'll find all kinds of ways to make and use them. When you experiment, it's a good idea to make a sample quilt from four fabric squares and

I'd rather use batting in the layers. Is that okay?

▶ Yes, but choose cotton batting—polyester will pull away in clumps instead of leaving soft, frayed edges within seams. Choose light or dark batting based on how you think the frays will look in exposed seams. Be sure to quilt an X or other shapes within blocks—that step isn't optional with regular batting because it needs the extra stabilization.

your chosen batting. Wash and dry the sample to preview the combination. Try some of these options in your rag quilts:

- Use low-loft cotton batting instead of flannel for even fluffier rag edges.
- Finish with a traditional binding instead of a rag outer edge.
- Make a quilt with other simple shapes, such as bars or rectangles.
- Use a 1" seam allowance for a different frayed look.
- Make a rag quilt accent pillow.
- Keep a denim rag quilt in the trunk of the car for cold-day emergencies.
- Make a soft rag quilt for your pets.
- Add border sandwiches to the quilt's edges using the same technique for sewing blocks.

Make a Larger Rag Quilt

Now that you've made one rag quilt, you'll find many ways to make more. Here are the yardages and pieces you need to make a quilt that finishes at 90" x 108". That's large enough to make a snuggly blanketlike quilt that drops far enough along the sides to tuck into most tall double mattresses. It will have a varying drop along the sides of larger mattress sizes.

Assemble the larger quilt in the same way you assembled the lap-sized version, but make twelve rows. Each row contains ten blocks. Measure your mattress's width, length, and depth. Change the block count if necessary for a better fit.

The quilt will become heavy as you assemble its rows. If you sew on a large table the quilt will have room to spread out as you add to it. If you sew at a small sewing station, where the quilt must hang off an edge of the table, the weight of the assembled

ELSEWHERE ON THE WEB

▶ You can use any type of sharp scissors to clip the seam allowances, but spring-action snips are much easier on your hands, and a good investment if you plan to make several rag quilts. Heritage Cutlery (www.heritage cutlery.com/quilting.html) makes spring-action snips with cushioned handles. The scissors are available from several mail order retailers, including Clotilde (www .clotilde.com). Keepsake Quilting (www.keepsakequilt ing.com) sells similar scissors that are perfect for trimming rag-quilt seams.

rows will pull on the needle, making it difficult to sew the quilt accurately. Solve the problem by keeping the already assembled rows rolled up to the left of the machine. Sometimes it's easier to handle heavy quilts if you throw the roll over your shoulder while you add the next row, rather than allowing it to rest to the left of the machine.

FABRIC REQUIREMENTS FOR LARGE QUILT

Position	Fabric	Yardage
Block fronts	Assorted flannels	8¾ yards
Backing	Flannel, homespun, or cotton prints	8¾ yards
Batting	Flannel	8¾ yards

CUTTING CHART FOR LARGE QUILT

Position	Patch Size	Number Required
Block fronts	10" x 10" square	120
Backing	10" x 10" square	120
Batting	10" x 10" square	120

Use these standard mattress sizes as a guide to make additional quilts. Knowing standard mattress lengths and widths will help you plan your quilt, but consider a few mattress variables before you make a final decision about quilt size. There are no standard mattress depths, and many of today's pillow-top versions are quite deep. Be sure to take depth into consideration when you choose a layout for your quilt.

- Decide how much width should extend past each side of the mattress.
- If you plan to use a dust ruffle, how large must the quilt be to extend past it in an attractive manner?
- Decide if you will let the quilt hang or tuck it in—and calculate drop length for the style you're looking for.
- Consider the bed's footboard when you design the quilt. If you plan to tuck it in under a footboard, consider making the bottom row shorter than the others to allow sides to hang.
- Will pillows be placed under it or on top of the quilt? Allow extra room at the top if you'll cover pillows and tuck them in.

STANDARD MATTRESS SIZES

Mattress Type	Size
Crib	28" x 52"
Twin/single	39" x 75"
Long twin	39" x 80"
Full/double	54" x 75"
Queen	60" x 80"
King	76" x 80"
California king	72" x 84"

Make a Strip-Pieced Rag Quilt

Here's a strip-pieced rag quilt that you can put together in an afternoon. The design is based on a traditional quilt block that's called either Roman Stripes or Rail Fence. Each block is made up of three long bars in color values of dark to light. Blocks are turned so that stripes in adjacent blocks are perpendicular to each other, and that arrangement creates a stair-step movement across the face of the quilt.

Fig. 12-3 Strip-pieced quilt layout ances

If you need a larger quilt, make additional strip sets. You can cut four blocks from each 42" long set. A spray baste product will keep strip layers together while you work, but straight pins are fine if spray baste is not available.

FINISHED QUILT AND BLOCK SIZES

Quilt Blocks	Finished Quilt
9" x 9"	45½" x 54½"

FABRIC REQUIREMENTS

Position	Fabric	Yardage
Block fronts	Dark cotton	I yard
Block fronts	Medium cotton	I yard
Block fronts	Light cotton	I yard
Block backs	Dark cotton	I yard
Block backs	Medium cotton	I yard
Block backs	Light cotton	I yard
Batting	Flannel	3 yards

Fabric	Position	Strip Size	Number Required
Dark fabric	Block fronts	4" x 42"	8
Medium fabric	Block fronts	4" x 42"	8
Light fabric	Block fronts	4" x 42"	8
Dark fabric	Block backs	4" x 42"	8
Medium fabric	Block backs	4" x 42"	8
Light fabric	Block backs	4" x 42"	8
Flannel	Batting	4" x 42"	32

Learn to strip piece the striped rag quilt. Before you begin, read the general instructions for strip piecing in Chapter 8. Some of the techniques differ for rag quilts, but seam allowance basics and the methods used to square up fabrics remain the same.

Here is how to strip piece the striped rag quilt:

1. Stack identical strips for block fronts in piles. Stack identical backing strips in piles. Stack batting strips in a pile.
2. Arrange a dark backing fabric strip right-side down on your sewing table. Place a batting strip on top of it, aligning all edges. Place a dark block front strip on top, right-side up. Secure the strips with several straight pins or use spray baste to keep the layers from shifting.
3. Make another strip sandwich, placing the medium backing right-side down on your sewing table, followed by the batting strip and the medium block front strip, which is placed right-side up. Secure strips.
4. Repeat to make another strip sandwich by combining the light backing, batting, and light block front strips. Secure.

5. Sew a dark strip sandwich lengthwise to a medium strip sandwich, placing backing sides together and using a ½" seam allowance.
6. Sew a light strip sandwich lengthwise to the medium strip sandwich, placing backing sides together and using a ½" seam allowance.
7. Finger press both seam allowances open. Press lightly with an iron to help the seams lay a bit flatter for cutting.

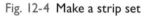

Fig. 12-4 **Make a strip set**

8. Use your rotary cutting equipment to square up one end of the strip set, then cut four 10" segments from it, starting with the squared-up end.
9. Combine the remaining fabric and batting strips in the same way and cut a total of thirty segments to create the striped blocks.

Now arrange the striped blocks into a quilt. Use the quilt layout drawing, Figure 12-1, to help you arrange the quilt blocks in rows. Layout the blocks as shown to begin with, just to get a feel for the movement created by dark to light bars. Then feel free to experiment with layouts until you find a design you love.

Here is how to arrange the striped blocks into a quilt:

1. Arrange the blocks on a design wall, placing them side by side to form six rows, each with five blocks. Position the left

block in the top row so that fabric stripes run vertically, with the darkest stripe on the left.

2. Place a block to the right of the first, with stripes running horizontally and the darkest stripe on top.

3. Repeat the arrangement, placing another vertically oriented block in the row next, followed by a horizontal block. Finish with a third vertical block.

4. Arrange five more blocks to create row 2, beginning and ending with stripes placed in a horizontal position.

5. Create four more rows, alternating block placement just as you did in the first two.

6. Step back and look at the quilt. Do the light and dark bars form a stair-step pattern down the quilt? If they don't, make sure the dark and stripes are oriented correctly—to the left for vertical blocks and along the top for horizontal blocks.

Sew the striped quilt blocks together. You'll sew the blocks together in no time at all—and that means you're almost finished! Try another Roman Stripe quilt, using completely different fabrics. You'll be surprised how much different the pattern looks with just that simple change.

Here is how to sew the striped quilt blocks together and finish the quilt:

1. Sew together the blocks in row 1, aligning backings together and using a ½" seam allowance. Finger press the seams open on the front of the blocks.

2. Use the same technique to sew together blocks in remaining rows.

3. Connect the rows together with a ½" seam allowance, aligning backing edges together carefully. Finger press seams open.
4. Sew a seam ½" inward from each side of the quilt.
5. Use sharp scissors to clip inward into all seam allowances, spacing clips about ¼" apart. Be careful not to clip the seam lines.
6. Wash and dry the quilt to create the frayed edges.

Get Linked

The Internet is a wonderful place to see every kind of quilt imaginable, from art quilts to vintage scrap quilts. The members of my About.com Quilting Forum have shared many of their quilts with readers. Stop by sometime and take a look, then stick around and try out a few of the projects in my quilt pattern library.

ONLINE QUILT SHOW

Lots of quilt galleries; all photos are submitted by members of the online quilting community. You'll find a everything from T-shirt quilts to landscapes.

http://about.com/quilting/galleries

EASY QUILTING PROJECTS

Plenty of patterns for complete quilts and quilt blocks, all suitable for beginning quilters.

http://about.com/quilting/easyquilts

The **ABOUT.com** *Guide to* **Quilting**

Chapter 13

Rag-Edged Denim Purse

Introduction to the Raggy Purse

Here's a fun and casual denim purse with lots of texture. You can cut out and sew the purse in a single day. There's no need to quilt the purse at all, and it will look fantastic even if your seam allowances aren't absolutely perfect because the seams are allowed to fray into softly raised lines between patches. Ragged-edge quilting offers another benefit, too—there's no need to sew a lining inside the purse. You'll automatically create a finished lining as you sew patches side by side. You'll find a photograph of the purse in this book's color insert.

You learned in Chapter 12 that rag quilts are made up of three layers, just like traditional quilts, but they're assembled in a completely different way. Patches are always aligned wrong sides together for sewing, leaving seam allowances exposed on the right side of the quilt. You'll find that it takes a bit of concentration to get into the habit of stitching with wrong sides aligned, since we're taught the exact opposite from the time we begin to sew. Read through the entire pattern before you begin to help you understand the process.

▶ Batik prints are a popular type of print created by first applying wax motifs to the surface of the fabric. The fabric is dyed, and the wax acts as a barrier to keep the color from changing in waxed areas. The wax is removed and more wax is applied in different areas before dyeing again. Formerly waxed areas pick up the dye, while new wax patterns shield the fabric. The process is repeated until the desired pattern and color scheme are achieved.

You'll need a rotary cutter, cutting mat, and 6" x 24" ruler to make the purse. Thin straight pins with round, visible tops are perfect for securing fabric edges when you sew pieces together. Other tools and supplies you'll need include a sewing machine equipped with a new denim needle, an iron and ironing board, cotton piecing thread, and a sharp lead pencil. A round pizza pan will help you mark curves on purse panels.

I chose lightweight denim for the outer layer of my purse. Denim frays nicely and I love its soft appearance. The bag's middle batting layer is flannel, another soft fabric that frays quite well. The backing pieces are cut from two different batik fabrics. Batiks aren't soft and they don't fray as much as the other two fabrics do, but their mottled colors mingle with the denim and flannel frays to create definition along the seams. If you don't have batiks, use any cotton fabric for the backing pieces.

FABRIC REQUIREMENTS

Fabric	Yardage
Lightweight denim	½ yard*
Flannel	¾ yard
Assorted nacking	¾ yard

*60" wide fabric

CUTTING CHART

Fabric	Patch Size	Number Required
Denim	3½" x 5½"	30
	3½" x 2¾"	10
	2" x 40"	1

Fabric	Patch Size	Number Required
Flannel	3½" x 5½"	30
	3½" x 2¾"	10
	2" x 40"	1
Backing pieces	3½" x 5½"	30
	3½" x 2¾"	10
	2" x 40"	1

Assemble the Pieced Rows

You'll find that this purse goes together more quickly when you chain piece, a technique that lets you sew one unit after another together in assembly-line fashion without removing pieces from the sewing machine or clipping threads. There's no need to worry about color placement if you're using assorted fabrics for the backing patches. Simply pull them from stacks in random order to create a wonderful scrappy lining.

Follow these steps to assemble the pieced rows:

1. Grab a 3½" x 5½" piece of denim and a flannel patch of the same size. Stack them together, placing the flannel rectangle against the denim piece's reverse side. Finish the stack by adding a backing patch of the same size, placing its reverse side against the flannel. Align all patch edges.
2. Make another stack using three more 3½" x 5½" denim, flannel, and backing rectangles.
3. Align the two stacks with each other, backing sides together. Sew a ½" seam to attach stacks along a short edge. Stop sewing when you reach the end of the patches but do not remove the unit from the sewing machine.

ELSEWHERE ON THE WEB

▶ Denim sewing needles have sharp points that help them pierce heavy, densely woven denim fabric. Start this project with a new denim needle and dispose of it when the project is finished, because it will become dull after traveling through many layers of fabric. The Schmetz Company's Web site offers a helpful description to help you choose sewing machine needles at www.schmetzneedles.com/ schmetz1.htm.

Fig. 13-1 **Two fabric stacks sewn on short sides**

▶ Quilters prefer long, thin straight pins with large heads that are visible on a wide variety of fabrics. Pins with bright yellow heads are available from most fabric stores. You'll also find pins with glow-in-the-dark heads—a handy component that makes dropped pins easy to find when you turn off the lights in your sewing room. Clover makes easy-to-spot straight pins with flat heads shaped like flowers. Try a box of each to see which straight pins you like best.

4. Make two more stacks and align the backing sides together. Slide them under or place them just in front of the sewing machine's presser foot. Begin sewing again and sew the new stack together just as you did the first, with ½" seam allowance. Stop at the edge of the patches but leave the unit in the sewing machine. That's all there is to chain piecing.

5. Continue chain piecing more stacked units together until you have ten units with two groups of 3½" x 5½" rectangles joined on a short side. Remove all of the units from the sewing machine and clip the threads between them.

6. Sew a third stacked group of 3½" x 5½" rectangles to a short end of each of the ten units.

7. Stack a 3½" x 2¾" piece of denim with flannel and backing pieces of the same size, placing the flannel in the middle with the wrong side of other fabrics touching it, just as you did the larger rectangles.

8. Align the shorter stack's longest edge with the short edge on either end of the previous units, wrong sides together. The edge lengths should match exactly. Sew together with a ½" seam allowance.

Fig. 13-2 **A finished row with three long units and one short unit**

9. Repeat to sew a shorter stack to each end of the remaining nine rows, chain piecing as before to save time and thread.

Assemble the Purse Front and Back

The front and back panels of the purse are each assembled from five of the rows you just finished sewing. The rows are arranged vertically, and shorter patches at row ends are flip-flopped from row to row to stagger the patches so you won't have to worry about matching seam intersections.

Follow these steps to assemble the purse front and back:

1. To make the purse front, gather five of the patchwork rows. Arrange them side by side near your sewing machine, the 3½" × 5½" patch units at the top. Turn the units in rows 2 and 4 around, so that the shorter denim rectangles are at the top.

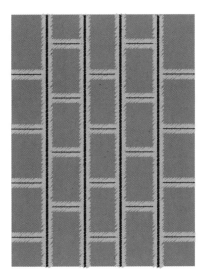

Fig. 13-3 Arrange five units in vertical rows

WHAT'S HOT

▶ Most quilters are so accustomed to sewing quarter-inch seams that sometimes it's difficult to switch to another width. A seam-allowance guide will help you remember where the edge of the fabric should be when you sew a seam. The guide can be as simple as a piece of masking tape placed on the throat plate of your sewing machine—most machines have grooved lines at the ½" position, so marking is a breeze.

2. Sew the rows together side by side, matching edges and placing backing sides together. Use straight pins to keep edges aligned as you sew.
3. Repeat with the remaining five rows to assemble the purse back.

Trim the Panels and Prepare the Strap

The bottom of the purse has rounded corners and the top of the purse has a rounded segment that curves inward at its center. All of the curves are easy to cut using a large, round pizza pan or other circular object as a template. It's easier to handle the panels and mark around the pan if you press the bulky seam allowances flat before you begin.

Here is how to trim the panels:

1. Place the purse front on your sewing table, backing-side up and oriented so that the short rectangles in rows 1, 2, and 3 are at the bottom. Place a round pizza pan near a bottom corner, centering and aligning its curve with the bottom and sides of the panel. The angular corners of the bag should extend beyond the curve. There is no right or wrong amount of curve to use, but removing just a small portion of the corner will result in a more spacious bag interior.

▶ If you have a walking foot for your sewing machine, put it on. A walking foot isn't a must for making rag quilts, but it is helpful. The special foot has built-in feed dogs that grip the top layer of the quilt and move it forward in unison with the sewing machine's lower feed dogs, advancing all layers at the same speed. The dual action helps reduce the shifting and bunching that can occur when sewing multiple layers of fabric.

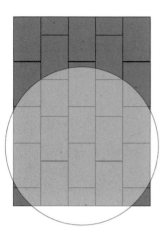

Fig. 13-4 Use a round pan to mark curves on bag panel

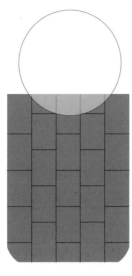

Fig. 13-5 Mark an inward curve at top of bag panel

ELSEWHERE ON THE WEB

▸ Elna, a Swiss company that makes sewing machines, offers a close-up photo of a walking foot on their Web site, www.elna.com/en/acces sories/sewing/walking, along with a short explanation of how it's used. Elna makes a standard walking foot and an open-toe walking foot, which has a wider opening that lets you see more of the project you are sewing.

2. Draw a line along the curves at each side.
3. Use sharp scissors to cut along each curve to remove the angular corners of the bag. Be sure to cut through all three layers of the front panel.
4. Use the front panel to mark the back panel, making sure you orient the back panel so that the short rectangles in rows 1, 3, and 5 are on the bottom. Cut to create curved edges.
5. Use the pizza pan, a plate, or other circular object to mark a gentle curve at the top center of each panel. Cut along marked lines.

It's time to try out the length of your purse strap. Place the 2" x 40" denim strip across your shoulder, centering it to hang evenly on each side. The end points indicate the approximate place the purse top will rest, but keep in mind that you'll lose about an

WHAT'S HOT

▶ Denim quilts are always popular and they add a casual look to any decor. You don't need a special pattern to make a denim quilt, and simple denim quilts are often the most striking. Working with denim is somewhat different than sewing with typical quilting cottons, so there are several factors you should consider that will help you sew a denim project together without a hitch. You'll find denim quilt tips and ideas on my Web site at http://about. com/quilting/denimquilts.

inch on each side for the seam allowance. Do you like where the strap ends? If the strap is too long, cut it back a bit and check again. Once you're satisfied with the length, cut the other long strap strips to match the denim strip.

Quilters sometimes add firmness to bag straps by fusing iron-on interfacing along their lengths. I wanted a soft strap, so I used only the three bag fabrics to make it. If you prefer a stiffer bag strap, cut a 1" wide segment of interfacing that's about an inch shorter than your strap length. Fuse it to the reverse side of the denim strip. Center the interfacing so that it won't intrude into the ½" side seam allowances that you'll sew in a bit and so that it stops approximately 1" from each end.

Here is how to prepare the strap:

1. Stack the three strap pieces together, placing the denim strip on top, right-side up, followed by the flannel strap and finishing with the backing strap, its reverse side against the flannel. Pin to keep edges from shifting.
2. Turn under one end of the strap by ½", denim sides together. Press. Turn again and press.
3. Stabilize the pressed end by sewing an X from one corner to the other within the turned area, then repeating for the other opposite corners.

Fig. 13-6 Sew an X to stabilize strap ends

4. Repeat, pressing under and sewing an X on the opposite end of the strap.

5. Sew a ½" seam along one long edge of the strap. Turn the strap around and sew another ½" seam along the opposite edge.

6. Use scissors to make perpendicular clips into the seam allowances all along the sides of the strap. Clip about every ¼" but take care not to clip into seam allowances. Set aside.

Finish Assembling the Purse

You're almost finished sewing! Just a few more seams and the pieces will begin to look like a purse. This is the point where I started to get excited and curious about the final look of the purse—and began to think about all of the other fabric combinations that would be suitable for this pattern. Reproduction prints are among my favorites and would be a lovely choice for this pattern.

Follow these steps to finish assembling the purse:

1. Place the purse front panel in the sewing machine. Sew a seam ½" from the top edge, starting and stopping about ¼" inward from each side. Backspace a few stitches at the beginning and end of the seam. Sew slowly to improve accuracy as you sew around the inward curve.

2. Repeat to sew a seam along the top edge of the purse's back panel.

3. Align the purse back and front, wrong sides together. Sew the sides and bottom of the purse together with a continuous ½" seam allowance. The top of the purse remains open.

4. Place one end of the strap near the top of the purse on one side, centering it with the midpoint of the side seam. The denim side of the strap should rest against the inside of the purse and the X stitches should be positioned just below

Is it okay to wash the purse with other items?

▶ Yes, it's fine to wash the purse with a few pieces of clothing or other items, just make sure not to pack the washer full since you want the water to flow around the seams to help fray them. Avoid washing a rag quilt with items that won't be dried in a dryer. The fluffing action of the dryer helps remove loose strings that become stuck to fabric.

the ½" seam you sewed along the top edge of each panel. Pin in place.

5. Sew the strap to the purse with two seams, one running along the top of the X and one along its bottom. Backstitch a short distance at the beginning and end of the seams.

6. Align the other end of the strap on the opposite side of the purse in the same way. Make sure the strap isn't twisted, then sew the strap to the purse.

Clip the seam allowances to make the purse ragged! The purse doesn't look ragged yet, does it? Not to worry—there are just a few more steps to take before the frayed edges appear. If you have a pair of rag-quilt scissors, now's the time to find them. These special scissors spring open every time you make a cut, and that keeps your hands from getting tired. The absence of thumb holes keeps your thumb from hurting, too. Another plus—rag-quilting shears have special tips to keep you from cutting into the seam allowance. If you don't have a special cutter, any sharp scissors will do.

Carefully cut straight into each exposed seam allowance, clipping through all layers of fabric about every quarter-inch but stopping before you reach a seam. Inspect allowances where seams meet to determine which direction to cut from. Clip these areas carefully to avoid removing large chunks of fabric.

When you've finished clipping, throw the purse into the washing machine on a long wash. I used three safety pins to secure the strap to the purse to help keep it from tangling during agitation. When the cycle is finished, place the purse in the dryer. It might take a bit longer than you expect to get it dry since there are multiple layers of fabric. I'll bet you can't resist opening the dryer at least once during the cycle to take a look—I couldn't.

Inspect the frayed edges. Did you forget to clip a seam? Clip it now. Turn the purse inside out and inspect the finished side. Are all of the seams intact? Frays that are visible on the finished side are a sign that the seam was damaged when you clipped the seam allowances. Turn the purse around again, back to the frayed side, and sew a new seam to repair the gap, beginning and ending a short distance from where the gap begins. Start and finish by backstitching to help keep the new seam intact. Some sewing machines can tie a knot at the beginning and end of a seam. Use that technique if it's available.

Trim away unruly threads and inspect the purse. Pop it back in the washer and dryer if you'd like for it to be more frayed or if you had to clip forgotten seam allowances. Inspect the purse for damaged seams after the second wash. Repair if necessary and trim loose threads.

Add a closure at the top of the purse if you like. A two-part, hook and loop closure like Velcro will work fine. Sew a short length of the stiff hook segment to one interior edge of the purse and a soft loop segment of the same length across from it on the inside of the other panel. Be sure to sew the closure below frayed edges so that frays won't be caught in the hooks. Protect the frays from the hook edge during a wash by placing a separate looped segment over it to keep other fabrics from sticking.

You can also center a button near the top center on one side of the bag, and then sew a fabric or corded loop on the front of the other panel, directly across from it. Wrap the loop around the button to close the purse.

That's it—you're finished! Make another purse if you like, varying the fabrics. Use quilting cottons on the outside instead of denim. Make the top and bottom curves a little deeper. Change its look in any way you like to suit your tastes.

ELSEWHERE ON THE WEB

▶ If you love purses and tote's, don't miss a trip to Linda McGeHee's Web site at www.ghees.com. Bags are one of her specialties and you'll find patterns for just about any style you can imagine—along with Linda's unique and colorful ideas for texture and embellishment. Ghee's also stocks colorful denims, threads, bag closures, and plenty of helpful notions.

Make a Quicker Rag Purse

You can put together a quick rag purse in no time at all by using three single panels of fabric instead of piecing panels with rectangles. The outer edges of this purse are ragged, and so are the handles. The inner and outer panels of the purse are solid fabrics, with no rags. Read through the entire pattern before beginning, because there are a few options to consider before you sew the purse together.

You'll need ½ yard each of denim, flannel, and lining fabric to make this version of the rag purse.

Follow these steps to make a quicker rag purse:

1. Cut two denim panels, each 12½" x 15".
2. Cut two lining panels and two flannel batting panels of the same size.
3. Place a lining panel right-side down on your work table. Center a batting panel on top of it, and then finish with a denim panel right-side up. Repeat to make another identical stack. Hold fabrics in each stack together with a few straight pins.
4. Refer back to the instructions for the first purse pattern in the section titled Trim the Panels and Prepare the Strap. Use those instructions to cut curves in the bottom and top of each stack.
5. Use the same previous instructions to prepare a strap for your purse.
6. Align the purse panels, lining sides together. Sew a ½" continuous seam beginning at the top of the purse on one side, curving around the bottom of the purse, and ending at the top of the opposite side. Backstitch at the beginning and end of the seam.
7. Starting at a side seam, sew a 1½" seam around the entire top edge of the purse. You're sewing through each panel inde-

▶ I used a light blue denim for my purse, but there are lots of other options. Visit fabric stores online and offline and you'll find all sorts of denims, including fabrics that look like old-fashioned mattress ticking. Try using more than one denim fabric to make the patchwork purse. Vary the strap and the optional pocket on the solid-panel purse. You won't need much fabric to make either one, so be sure to look for unusual denims on the remnant tables at your favorite fabric shops.

pendently here—not connecting them with a seam allowance. Backstitch at the beginning and end of the seam.

8. Add the handle to the purse as directed in the previous instructions.

9. Clip the seams as you did with the pieced purse. Wash and dry the purse to encourage fraying.

Consider these options for your quick rag purse. If you would like to add quilting stitches or a pocket you must do that before the stacked panels are sewn together. Use straight-line or free-motion quilting to add interest to the plain denim panel. Variegated threads that move from pearly white to dark blue would look very good stitched in large, free-motion curves.

To add a pocket, cut a square or rectangle from each fabric. The size is up to you. Stack the fabrics as you did the purse panels and use a small circular object to mark curves along the bottom edge. Leave the top edge straight. Hold the stack together with a pin.

Position the stack on one side of the purse. Move it around until you find the best spot for it. If the pocket is too large, simply trim it back. Try flipping the pocket over so that the lining is visible on the front of the purse. Do you like that look better?

Once you've decided on a size, sew a ½" seam across the top edge of the pocket, starting and stopping ½" from each side. Backstitch at the beginning and ending of the seam.

Place the pocket back on the purse panel and sew it in place with a continuous seam around its sides and bottom. Begin sewing at the top of one side corner and continue on to the opposite side. Backstitch at the beginning and end of the seam. Use your scissors to make perpendicular clips into the pocket's seam allowances. Finish the purse as directed.

There are many other ways to customize this purse. Use the string-piecing skills you learned in Chapters 8 and 11, making front panels that are covered with strings. Sew on buttons, lace, or silk ribbon. Add machine embroidery motifs to the denim. Sew on beads. Brainstorm a bit and you'll come up with ideas that make this purse your very own design.

Get Linked

You'll find patterns and other resources to help you create more purses and tote bags on my About.com Quilting Web site.

PURSE AND TOTE PATTERNS

An index of tote bags and purse patterns, from simple to advanced; there's something here for everyone.

http://about.com/quilting/pursesandtotes

EMBELLISHING YOUR QUILTING PROJECTS

Use these resources to learn to apply cording, paint with thread, paint your fabrics, embroider special stitches, and more.

http://about.com/quilting/embellishments

SEWING MACHINE ACCESSORIES

Here's a handy photo gallery that includes a variety of sewing machine accessories, including a walking foot, seam guides, stitch regulators, sewing surfaces, and lots of other helpful tools. The gallery includes tips to help you select and use each type of tool.

http://about.com/quilting/sewingmachineaccessories

Chapter 14

Basket Wall Hanging and Throw Pillow

Basket Quilt Introduction

You can sew this easy basket wall hanging in one weekend—and without using very much fabric. The quilt is made up of a large basket block that's assembled with quick-piecing techniques. The basket is set on point and surrounded by triangles. Two borders complete the quilt's outer edges. The basket quilt makes a wonderful, quick gift. It looks nice on a wall, but it would also be good at home thrown over the back of a comfy chair or centered on a small table.

About.

Fig. 14-1 **Basket quilt layout**

You won't need lots of different fabrics to make the basket quilt. Fabrics that will be sewn next to each other should vary in color value—enough to make the division between patches noticeable, but the variance does not need to be extreme. Review the information about color value in Chapter 2, and remember that your dark starting point can be lighter than the quilt shown in the illustration.

You'll need a rotary cutter, cutting mat, and 6" x 24" ruler to make this quilt. A 15" square ruler will help you make sure the basket block is square. Thin straight pins are perfect for securing fabric edges when you sew pieces together. Other tools and supplies you'll need include a sewing machine, iron and ironing board, cotton piecing thread, and a sharp lead pencil. You'll need a pillow form to make the optional pillow, plus a few safety pins and a piece of flannel that matches the size of the pillow.

You can sew this little quilt in the watercolor style. If you're not familiar with watercolor quilts, think about impressionistic paintings—you don't always see the image the artist has drawn when you inspect it up close, but the picture emerges when you view it from a distance. Watercolor quiltmaking helps you create a similar look in cloth. The technique was called colorwash by its original developer, British quilter Dierdre Armsden.

Traditional watercolor quilts are made from hundreds of pieces of floral fabrics, often 2½" squares. Patches are typically arranged on a design wall one by one, with the quiltmaker stepping back often to view the layout then returning to rearrange components until the desired effect is achieved. The technique became so popular during the 1990s that fabric shops began to sell precut floral patches in bundles to help quilters build their stash of watercolor fabric without buying large chunks of fabric.

Fabrics with large, open spaces between floral motifs generally don't work as well for watercolor quilts, but a larger-scale print would be fine for the triangles that surround our little basket block. Choose busier fabrics for other patches—with overall floral motifs that seem to melt into each other.

If you don't like florals, feel free to sew the quilt with other fabrics. How about a Christmas theme, or maybe a mixture of blues and yellows? You'll find two examples of the finished basket quilt in this book's color insert—one a full quilt and the other a basket block used to create a throw pillow.

BASKET QUILT FINISHED SIZES

Basket Block	**Finished Quilt**
15" x 15"	37½" x 37"

ELSEWHERE ON THE WEB

▶ There are hundreds of fabric shops online, and since floral fabrics are one of the most popular quilting fabrics, it should be easy to find prints that you like. A few of my favorite online quilting supply stores are The Virginia Quilter (www.virginia quilter.com), Keepsake Quilting (www.keepsakequilting .com), and Hickory Hill Quilts (www.hickoryhillquilts .com).

Fabric	Position	Yardage
Very light	Large corner triangles	⅜ yard
Medium light	Basket background	⅓ yard
Medium	Basket base and legs	11" x 15" scrap
Medium dark	Inner border	½ yard
Dark	Outer border	¾ yard
Very dark	Basket handle and binding	½ yard
Any fabric	Backing	1⅛ yard

CUTTING CHART

Fabric Position	Patch Size	Number Required
Corner triangles	11½" x 11½"	2
Basket background	9⅞" square	1
	3⅞" square	4
	3½" x 9½" bars	2
Basket base	9⅞" x 9⅞"	1
	3⅞" x 3⅞"	1
Inner border	3½" x 42"	4
Outer border	5½" x 42"	4
Basket handle	3⅞" x 3⅞"	4

Keep the basket block in mind for a throw pillow. You'll find instructions for a basket block accent pillow near the end of this chapter. To make the basket pillow, you'll need the same amount of medium light fabric for the basket background that is required for the quilt, the medium fabric for the basket base, and a 16" square of

ASK YOUR GUIDE

Where can I see examples of watercolor quilts?

▶ There are hundreds of pictures of watercolor quilts on the Internet. I maintain a library of watercolor Web sites at http://about.com/ quilting/watercolorsites. You'll find more examples of watercolor quilts by searching the phrases watercolor quilt and color wash quilt on Google (www.google.com). Several books have been written about the method, including *Watercolor Quilts*, by Pat Maixner Magaret and Donna Ingram Slusser, and *Quick Watercolor Quilts: the Fuse, Fold and Stitch Method*, by Dina Pappas.

very dark fabric for the basket handle. Border and backing amounts vary, so read the pattern before purchasing yardages.

Make the Basket Handle Units

The basket handles are made from half-square triangle units. You'll use this popular unit in the majority of the quilts you make. Because the units are so popular, there are lots of ways to construct them. The directions here step you through one of my favorite methods, a simple technique that uses squares of fabric that are sewn together along the diagonal, and then cut apart to create the triangle square units.

Follow these steps to make the basket handle units:

1. Gather the 3⅞" very dark and medium light squares. Use a pencil or permanent marker to draw a diagonal line on the reverse side of each medium light square, from one corner to the opposite corner.
2. Sandwich a lighter and darker square, right sides together and edges matched carefully. Hold the patches together with a few straight pins along their edges to keep the fabrics from shifting apart.
3. Sew two seams to attach the squares, placing each seam ¼" outward from the lightest square's premarked center line. Use a rotary ruler to mark sewing lines if you are not using a quarter-inch presser foot. Press the unit flat, just as it was sewn.
4. Use scissors or rotary cutting equipment to cut the patches apart along the drawn line. Place the two new units on your ironing board, darkest side up. Flip the dark triangle up, opening it with your fingers and pressing it back gently, using your nails to separate fabrics along the seam. Press carefully with the iron. Clip off the little triangular "dog ears"

that extend past the unit where seams end at two corners. Repeat to complete the second triangle square unit.

5. The finished half-square triangle units, also called triangle squares, should measure exactly 3½" × 3½". If they are too small, try pressing again. If the units are still too small, sew the next pair with a slightly narrower seam allowance or use the instructions in Chapter 8 to verify that you are sewing an exact ¼" seam.

6. Combine the remaining 3⅞" squares in the same way to assemble a total of eight triangle square units. Only seven are needed for the basket, but hang on to the extra if you like, because triangle squares are one of the most commonly used quilting components.

Finish Assembling the Basket Block

It doesn't take long to finish assembling the basket block. Work carefully and be sure to sew an accurate ¼" seam allowance. Press after each step and your block will be perfect.

Follow these steps to finish assembling the basket block:

1. Gather the 9⅞" squares, one medium for the basket base and one medium light background piece. Use rotary equipment to carefully cut each one in half once diagonally, from one corner to the opposite corner.

2. Align the squares right sides together, edges matched. Sew a ¼" seam along their longest edge. Finish the large triangle square unit exactly as you did the smaller basket handle units, pressing the seam allowance toward the darkest fabric. Trim dog ears at seam ends.

3. Cut the 3⅞" medium fabric square in half once diagonally. Sew the short side of a square to one end of a 3½" × 9½" bar as illustrated in the basket assembly diagram, Figure 14-2.

ELSEWHERE ON THE WEB

▶ I mentioned Thangles—preprinted sheets of paper that help you sew flawless half-square triangle units—earlier in the book. The folks at Thangles maintain an online quilt gallery where you'll find all sorts of inspiration for using the units in your quilts. Visit http://thangles.com/gallery.htm.

Sew the second triangle to the remaining bar, placing it in a mirror image configuration as shown.

Fig. 14-2 **Basket assembly diagram**

4. Find the medium light 9⅞" triangle left over from the basket base assembly. Use rotary cutting equipment to trim it back along the long edge, leaving short sides that are 7" long.
5. Arrange the block components next to your sewing machine as shown in the basket assembly diagram.
6. Sew the triangle units together into two rows as shown. One row contains three units and the remaining row has four. Press seam allowances toward the darker triangles.
7. Sew the three-unit triangle square row to the side of the basket, taking care to orient the triangle squares as illustrated. Press the seam allowance toward the large background triangle.
8. Sew the remaining triangle square row to the unit created in step 3. Press the seam allowance toward the large background triangle.
9. Sew a bar/triangle unit to each side of the block, orienting them so that the short side of each bar's dark triangle touches the basket base as shown. Press seam allowances toward the bars.

TOOLS YOU NEED

▶ A large square rotary ruler makes it a breeze to check the sizes of your quilt blocks and other pieced units. Put the clear ruler on top of the block to see how it lines up with the grid. Two of my favorite brands of rulers are Olfa and Omnigrid, but there are many others. If you're new to rotary cutting, drop by a local quilt shop and ask for a ruler demo so that you can see them close up.

10. Fold the remaining background triangle in half along its longest edge to find the midpoint. Center it right-side down along the base of the basket, raw edges aligned. Sew the triangle to the basket and press the seam allowance toward the new triangle. Its sides will extend slightly past the sides of the basket block.
11. Use your rotary equipment to trim the oversized triangle even with both sides of the quilt block.
12. The basket block should measure 15½" square. If it's smaller, press again to make sure all seams are fully open.
13. Cut each 11½" very light square in half once diagonally to produce four large triangles.
14. Fold a triangle in half along its longest edge and finger crease. Match the crease to the midpoint along one side of the basket block, right sides together and edges aligned. Sew together. Press the seam allowance toward the large triangle.
15. Crease each remaining large triangle. Sew a triangle to the opposite side of the block, then to the two remaining sides, pressing seam allowances toward the triangles after each is added. Trim off the little dog ears that extend past block sides where triangle ends meet.

Sew on the Borders and Finish the Quilt

Adding borders is one of the final steps you must take before sandwiching and quilting the quilt. Refer back to Chapter 4 to learn how to measure and cut borders for your quilt. If the quilt is slightly skewed, your borders can help bring it back into shape.

Here is how to sew on the borders and finish the quilt:

1. Gather the 3½" × 42" strips reserved for inner borders. Measure for side borders as directed in Chapter 4 and cut two borders that length. Sew them to the sides of the quilt as explained in the instructions. Press seam allowances toward the borders.
2. Measure, cut, and sew the top and bottom inner borders to the quilt in the same way.
3. Use the same method to cut and sew the 5½" × 42" strips to the quilt to create outer borders.
4. Refer to the instructions in Chapter 9 to finish the quilt. You'll mark the top for quilting if necessary, sandwich it with batting and backing, hand or machine quilt it, then sew mitered binding to the quilt's edges with a ¼" seam. Be sure to add a hanging sleeve so that it's easy to display the quilt on a wall. You'll find hanging sleeve instructions in Chapter 10.

A quilt label makes another nice finishing touch. Consider personalizing your quilt by adding a label to its backing fabric. You'll find all sorts of labels online and at your local quilt shop, all printed side by side on fabric that you can purchase by the yard. If you prefer, you can also design and print your own unique labels using a computer and inkjet printer.

A permanent label dates your quilt for future generations. Be sure to add a little information about you, the recipient, and the reason it was made—especially if the quilt was a gift. Be sure to use a permanent marker to write on the label.

Turn under the edges of the label and use a straight or decorative machine stitch to sew it securely to the backing before you sandwich the three layers of the quilt. An alternative is to piece the backing and add the label as one of your fabric patches.

▶ I rarely use solid fabrics in my quilts, opting instead for tone on tones, which resemble solids from a distance but are actually printed with varying versions of one color. This pillow is an exception, because I think it would look lovely sewn with a black background and vibrantly colored solid basket components.

My basket block is skewed. Why did that happen?

▶ Sometimes it's difficult to sew stretchy components together without stretching them out of shape. To fix this, I recommend that you cut a piece of freezer paper 15½" square. Mark strategic points of the block on the paper, such as the center and correct position of rows. Press the paper to your ironing board and center the block on top. Which sides are off? Coax the block into shape, holding it in place with straight pins. Press, using a bit of spray starch to help the block retain its shape. Cut and add the borders.

Make a Basket Throw Pillow

It's easy to make a decorative pillow from the basket block. Use the block alone, without the surrounding triangles that are sewn to it in the quilt, to make a 15" square pillow. You can purchase pillow forms at fabric shops and craft stores. Since the basket block won't be surrounded by triangles, its sides will be parallel to the sides of the pillow form. Sew the large triangles to the block if you want to make a larger pillow—about 21" square.

Add a narrow border to the block if you prefer to make a pillow that's only slightly larger than the block. Determine how much extra width and length you need to fit the pillow form and add ½" to the width of each strip to compensate for seam allowances. For instance, to make a 16" pillow, cut 1" wide strips for the border. Sew a border to each side of the block just as you would for a quilt.

Decide if you want to quilt the basket block or leave it as it is. Flannel makes an excellent batting for quilted patchwork pillows, adding a little depth without making them too bulky. Cut a flannel square with sides that are ½" shorter than your quilt block so that the flannel doesn't add bulk to seam allowances. Center the flannel on the back of the block and press the two together. Secure with a few safety pins pinned through from the top, avoiding areas where you plan to quilt if possible.

Do a little simple straight-line machine quilting along seams or add gentle curves to open areas of the block. You should be able to use your regular presser foot to machine quilt the block, but if you have a walking foot, put it on your sewing machine. Remove safety pins as necessary to quilt. You'll find machine-quilting basics in Chapter 9.

Now let's make the back of the pillow. I'm not great with zippers, so I love this easy pillow method that lets me slip the pillow form in and out of the cover through an overlapped opening on its back.

Here is how to construct the pillow cover:

1. Cut a pillow back that matches the height of your pillow front but is 5" longer. For instance, if you are making the basket block without a border, the front should be 15½" square. Add 5" to one side and cut a rectangular back that measures 15½" x 20½".
2. Fold the back in half, matching short edges. Crease along the fold.
3. Use your rotary cutting equipment to cut the pillow back fabric in half along the crease.
4. Turn under the cut edge of one back piece by ½". Press neatly. Turn it under again by the same amount and press. Use a matching thread to machine stitch a seam close to the first folded edge. Repeat to fold under and sew the trimmed edge of the second backing piece.

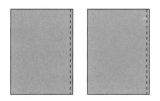

Fig. 14-3 Turn under and sew edges of backing pieces

5. Place the basket block right-side up on your sewing table. Place one of the backing fabrics on top of the basket, right-side down and outer, raw edges matched to the basket block's edges. The seamed edge should be positioned to run up and down in a vertical line. Pin edges to keep fabrics from shifting.

ELSEWHERE ON THE WEB

▶ Pillow forms are available at discount stores, such as Wal-Mart, and craft stores like Michaels and Ben Franklin. Your local quilt and fabric shops might also carry pillow forms. Mountain Mist, a quilt batting company, carries a nice line of pillow forms in many sizes. View their products online at www.stearns textiles.com/products.htm. Fairfield is another quilt batting company that makes pillow forms in many sizes. Read about their pillows online at www.poly-fil.com/pillows.asp.

6. Place the second backing fabric on the opposite side of the block, right-side down and raw, outer edges aligned. The seamed edge should be vertical and overlapping the seamed edge of the first backing piece.
7. Attach the backing pieces to the basket block by sewing a ¼" seam along the entire length of each outer edge.

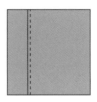

Fig. 14-4 **Assemble the pillow cover**

8. Trim away little triangular shapes at each corner of the pillow cover to reduce bulk. Turn the pillow cover right-side out and use your fingers to smooth it at the seam allowances. Insert the pillow form through the overlapped opening on the pillow back and you're finished!

You can add yo-yos to the basket to mimic flowers. Yo-yos are rosettes that are made by gathering circles of fabric. They are usually sewn side by side into rows to create quilts and coverlets, but they also make quick and easy dimensional flowers—perfect for our basket pillow. Finished yo-yos will be about half the size of the fabric circle you start with. I used two sizes to make mine, 5½" circles and 4" circles. Use a small plate or other round object to mark and cut fabric.

Here is how to add yo-yos to your basket quilt or pillow:

▶ You can make a quick accent pillow by cutting a pillow back to match the size of the pillow front. Place the two right sides together and sew a seam along three sides. Clip the corners to reduce bulk and turn the unit right-side out. Turn under the raw edges along the open side and hand sew close with matching thread. Keep in mind that, although this method is fast, it makes it more difficult to wash the pillow.

1. Cut out an assortment of fabric circles.
2. Thread a hand-sewing needle with quilting thread. If you use regular thread, sew with two strands to add strength.
3. Knot the end of the thread. Fold under the edge of the circle by about ¼" and bring the needle up through the seam allowance to the top of the circle.
4. Continue sewing around the circle, folding the seam allowance as you sew. Your seam allowance needn't be perfect.
5. When you reach the starting point, pull on the thread to gather the circle into a rosette. Distribute the gathers, leaving a small hole in the center of the rosette.
6. Secure the thread with a few backstitches, then knot. Repeat to make more yo-yos.

Arrange the yo-yos in the basket, with holes facing you and letting some overlap others. Appliqué the yo-yos to the fabric. Use enough stitches to hold the yo-yos in place, but it's not necessary to sew all the way around each one.

You can dress up the yo-yos by sewing a decorative bead or button at the center of each one—over the opening. Another option is to turn the yo-yos around, with the holes facing the background fabric. If you use that method, try taking a few stitches in the back of each yo-yo when you secure the gathered seam. Pull the stitches slightly to create a small tuck at the center of each circle to make the yo-yos look more like dimensional flowers.

WHAT'S HOT

▶ If you like larger pillows, go ahead and add the four triangles to the sides of the basket block to make a square pillow cover that's just a tiny bit larger than 21" x 21". You should be able to find a 21" square pillow form. I like to use inserts that are soft and comfortable, rather than rigid pillows that are strictly for looks.

Get Linked

There are lots of ways to make quick-pieced units like the easy triangle squares we sewed for the basket block. You'll find more techniques for easy piecing on my About.com Quilting site.

HOW TO CUT PATCHWORK SHAPES

Cutting specific patchwork shapes is sometimes the first step for quick piecing your quilts.

↗ http://about.com/quilting/cuttingshapes

MAKING AND USING YO-YOS

More details about yo-yos, including photos of yo-yo quilts and coverlets.

↗ http://about.com/quilting/yoyoquilts

Chapter 15

Shades of the Past: A Vintage-Look Quilt

Vintage-Look Quilt Introduction

This easy-to-make little quilt is stitched in fabrics that are reproductions of prints from the 1920s to 1930s. Nine-patch blocks are set on point and linked together with Snowball blocks—large squares with triangles at their tips. Half-Snowball blocks replace the traditional, plain setting triangles typically used along an on-point quilt's outer edges.

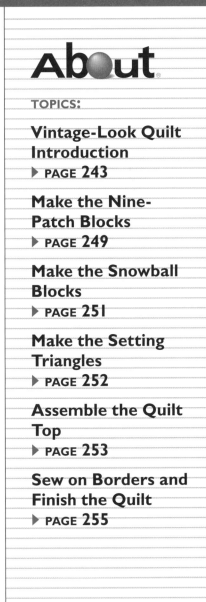

About.

Fig. 15-1 Vintage-style quilt layout

Now it's time to choose colors and fabrics. Cotton fabrics from the 1920s and 1930s are similar, but they did change somewhat in appearance throughout the period. Pastel solid and printed fabrics were fashionable in 1920s and replaced the dark, subdued colors of past eras. White fabric printed with black geometric designs was another popular choice for quilters during that period.

Geometric prints were a staple in the 1920s—dots, squares, diamonds, and other similar shapes, printed alone or in combination with each other. Juvenile prints were introduced, including fabrics with drawings of children running and playing and doing other things that children like to do. Cats, dogs, and other animals were another popular choice of the 1920s era. Floral prints were plentiful, but they were usually fairly simple drawings, not the realistic florals we see printed on fabric today.

Printed stripes and plaids were popular. So were woven examples of those two themes—where threads of different colors are intertwined to create the design. Solid fabrics were available to coordinate with prints.

The 1930s were ushered in by the stock market collapse and resulting economic depression, a time when homemakers learned to be even more frugal than they had in the past. Feed and grain companies began to sell all sorts of bulk foods in brightly printed cotton sacks that could be used to make clothing and quilts after the product was consumed. Feedsacks from the early twentieth century are still popular today and can be found in antique shops, online stores, and on auctions such as eBay.

We saw a progression toward brighter and darker colors in the 1930s, and fabrics were more likely to be printed from multiple colors than they were just ten years before. Bright greens and pinks were characteristic of the time, and colors were combined that don't really seem to match. Prints were larger and more complex than the simple shapes of the 1920s. Geometrics were still around, but floral designs of all types were more common.

The Internet has made it possible to easily view vintage quilts and fabrics—or find reproductions. You'll find resources to help you select reproduction fabrics in Appendix B.

You'll need a rotary cutter, cutting mat, and 6" × 24" ruler to make this quilt. A 12" square ruler is helpful for making sure blocks are square. Thin straight pins are perfect for securing fabric edges when you sew pieces together. Other tools and supplies you'll need include a sewing machine, iron and ironing board, cotton thread, and a sharp lead pencil.

The quilt is assembled using rotary cutting methods combined with quick-piecing and strip-piecing techniques. Refer back to Chapters 6 and 7 for details about each method. You'll use ¼" seams throughout the quilt.

Now let's take a look at the positions of colors and color values. The quilt layout drawing, Figure 15-1, pictured at the beginning of this chapter shows you where light and dark colors

WHAT'S HOT

▶ If you look for feedsacks on www.eBay.com, try searching several terms: feedsacks, feed sacks, feed bags, and flour sacks often provide different results. Advertising feedsacks and bags with pictorial images are usually the most expensive. Sacks that depict children always seem to be popular. You'll find a variety of listings, from partial bags to full bags that are still stitched along their sides. Some feedsacks still have paper labels attached.

ASK YOUR GUIDE

Where can I find reproduction quilting fabrics?

▶ Several quilting fabric designers and manufacturers specialize in recreating fabrics from past eras. The Aunt Grace Scrapbag collection, by Judie Rothermel for Marcus Brothers Textiles, is one example of fabrics that are excellent reproductions of early twentieth-century prints and colors. Aunt Grace Scrapbag fabrics are available at many local and online quilt shops. You'll find the company's Web address, and a list of more fabric manufacturers, in Appendix B.

are positioned in the quilt. Remember that dark fabrics move forward in the design to catch our eye and that a warm color usually stands out more than a cool color. You can use the differences in color value and color warmth to make some areas of the quilt pop out and others recede.

Refer back to Chapter 2, Working with Fabrics and Colors, if you need a little help with color selection. If you'd like a bit more inspiration, take a look at the color photos of this quilt located in the color inset. One example is sewn with reproduction fabrics and the other is made from very contemporary batiks.

Nine-patch and Snowball quilt blocks have both been popular for a very long time, so if you're not a fan of early twentieth-century fabrics, choose fabrics from another era. Civil War prints would suit this quilt perfectly and are available from many fabric manufacturers. If you love contemporary prints, use those. The quilt will work with any fabric theme you choose.

FINISHED QUILT AND BLOCK DIMENSIONS

Nine-Patch Blocks	Snowball Blocks	Finished Quilt
9" x 9"	9" x 9"	55½" x 55½"

FABRIC AND BATTING REQUIREMENTS

Location Letter	Fabric Type	Fabric Placement	Yardage
A	Very dark print	Nine-patch centers, narrow border, binding	¾ yard
B	Dark print	Nine-patch squares, wide border	1⅔ yard
C	Medium dark print	Nine-patch squares	¼ yard

D	Medium print	Snowball block centers	⅓ yard
E	Light print	Snowball block tips	⅓ yard
F	Medium light print	Setting and corner triangles	⅝ yard
	Backing fabric		2½ yards
	Thin quilt batting		62" x 62" square

CUTTING CHART

Location Letter	Fabric Type	Fabric Placement	Cutting Instructions
A	Very dark print	Nine-patch blocks	Cut one 3½" x 34" strip
		Inner border	Cut four 2" x 42" strips
		Binding	Cut six 2" x 42" strips
B	Dark print	Nine-patch blocks	Cut one 3½" x 42" strip
			Cut one 3½" x 27" strip
			Cut two 3½" x 34" strips
		Outer border	Cut five 7½" x 42" strips
C	Medium dark print	Nine-patch blocks	Cut one 3½" x 42" strip
			Cut one 3½" x 27" strip

Location Letter	Fabric Type	Fabric Placement	Cutting Instructions
D	Medium print	Nine-patch blocks	Cut one 3½" x 42" strip
			Cut one 3½" x 27" strip
		Snowball block centers	Cut one 9½" x 42" strip
E	Light print	Snowball block tips	Cut two 3½" x 42" strips
F	Medium light print	Setting triangles	Cut one 14" x 29" strip
		Corner triangles	Cut one 7¼" x 15" strip

TOOLS YOU'LL NEED

▶ If you're a beginning quilter, you might wonder which tools you really need to make a quilt. The short answer is it depends. Do you want to make pieced quilts or appliqué quilts? Some of the tools required for each type of project are the same, but there are lots of little specialty tools to help you complete specific tasks quickly and accurately. You'll find a complete list of basic tools in Chapter 1 and details about specialty tools throughout the book.

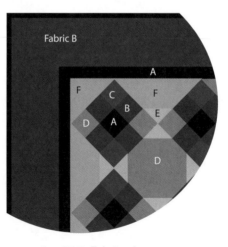

Fig. 15-2 **Fabric placement**

Make the Nine-Patch Blocks

Assemble the nine-patch blocks first because they're quick and easy. Before you begin, make sure you're sewing an accurate ¼" seam. Refer to Chapter 7 to learn how to check your seam allowance, and correct it if necessary. If you're a new quilter, brush up on strip-piecing basics in the same chapter.

Here is how to assemble the nine-patch blocks:

1. Gather the six dark, medium dark, and medium print strips you cut for nine-patch blocks. Sort the strips into two groups of matching lengths. One group is made up of three 3½" × 42" strips, and the other is made up of three 3½" × 27" strips.

2. Sew the three 3½" × 42" strips together lengthwise to create a strip set, placing the darkest fabric in the center. Press the seam allowance toward the center strip.

3. Use your rotary cutting equipment to square up one end of the strip set, then cut twelve 3½" long segments from the squared-up end. If you can only cut eleven, don't worry—you can cut an extra segment from the shorter strip set you'll make next. Check occasionally to be sure the end of your strip set remains square.

ELSEWHERE ON THE WEB

▶ The Kirk Collection specializes in vintage textiles, and proprietor Nancy Kirk has compiled a video to help you date vintage fabrics at www.kirkcollection.com/datingfabrics.html. The video's wonderful for that task, but it also helps you determine which reproduction fabrics suit specific eras. Take some time to read Nancy's Web site if you'd like to learn more about vintage fabrics.

Fig. 15-3 Make the first strip set and cut segments

4. Sew the 3½" x 27" strips together in the same way, with the darkest strip in the center. Square up one end of the strip set and cut six 3½" long segments from it. You should now have eighteen identical segments. Stack them together.

5. Gather the remaining strips cut for nine-patch blocks, one very dark and two medium dark strips measuring 3½" x 34".

6. Sew the strips together lengthwise, placing the very dark strip in the center. Press the seam allowances toward the side strips.

7. Use your rotary cutting equipment to square up one end of the strip set, then cut nine 3½" segments from it. Stack segments together.

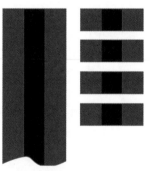

Fig. 15-4 **Make the second strip set and cut segments**

8. Gather two segments from the step 4 stack and one segment from your step 7 stack. Arrange the segments into three rows, with the very dark/dark segment in the center row. Orient the two outer, identical segments so that end patches are in mirror image positions from each other.

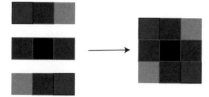

Fig. 15-5 **Arrange nine-patch rows and sew together**

9. Sew the rows together, matching seams carefully.
10. Repeat steps 8 and 9 to make a total of nine nine-patch blocks. Set aside.

A large, square rotary ruler helps you make sure you've assembled accurate blocks. The 12" and 15" rulers are large enough to help you check a variety of block sizes. Square rulers are divided into grids with markings every ⅛" along their sides—you simply place a ruler on top of a block to evaluate its components. Check your nine-patch blocks now. Each one should measure 9½" square, with no edges that skew away from that dimension.

Make the Snowball Blocks

I always use this quick-piecing technique to assemble Snowball blocks. It lets me sew squares to the corners of the snowballs, then trim them back to create triangles, and that means I never have to work with stretchy bias edges. Eliminating stretch during assembly is one of the best ways I know to make accurate blocks.

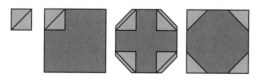

Fig. 15-6 **Making the Snowball blocks**

TOOLS YOU NEED

▶ Visit a quilt shop and you'll find all sorts of marking pens and pencils, including lead pencils that make dark or light lines, permanent markers of every color, chalk markers, and pens with pale inks that disappear over time or when water touches them. For the method we're using on this quilt, drawn lines aren't visible after the quilt block is assembled, so feel free to mark your squares with any type of pen or pencil that won't rub off onto nearby fabric.

Follow these steps to make the snowball blocks:

1. Gather the light 3½" × 42" strips reserved for Snowball block tips. Use your rotary cutting equipment to square up one end of each strip, then cut a total of twenty-four 3½" squares from it.
2. Using a straight edge and pencil, draw a diagonal line from one corner to the other on the reverse side of each 3½" square. If the fabric drags and distorts under the pencil, mark the square in two motions. Start midway along the diagonal and mark outwards, then finish by marking from the midpoint to the opposite diagonal. Set aside.
3. Find the 9½" × 42" strip reserved for Snowball block centers. Square up one end of the strip, then cut four 9½" squares from it.
4. Align a marked light square with one corner of a 9½" medium square, right sides together and edges matched. Sew a seam on the small square's marked line. Repeat, sewing a small square to each corner of the large square.
5. Press the seams flat, just as they were sewn, then trim away both layers of excess fabric between the seam line and the matched corners, taking care to leave an approximate ¼" seam allowance.
6. Press the ¼" seam allowances toward the large square. Press carefully to avoid stretching the triangles.
7. Repeat to make a total of four Snowball blocks.

Make the Setting Triangles

Setting triangles fill in the gaps around the quilt's side blocks. They're often made with plain triangles, but we'll add a little more interest by sewing a small triangle to a corner of each one. The little triangles help link the setting triangles to the Snowball blocks, adding an extra bit of visual movement to the pattern.

Follow these steps to make the setting triangles:

1. Square up one end of the 14" × 19" medium light strip, then cut two 14" × 14" squares from it.
2. Use your rotary cutting equipment to cut each square in half twice diagonally to form eight triangles with the fabric's straight grain along their longest edge.

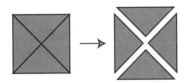

Fig. 15-7 **Cut setting triangles from large squares**

3. Sew a light square to a setting triangle using the same technique you used to sew squares to Snowball blocks. Place the square in the corner where the triangle's two short edges meet. Repeat to make eight identical setting triangles.

Fig. 15-8 **Make the setting triangles**

Assemble the Quilt Top

Shades of the Past is assembled by arranging its components into diagonal rows, sewing the blocks in each row together, then joining the rows. Corner triangles are the last pieces you'll sew to the quilt top.

Can't I just measure each edge of the quilt and cut border strips to match the lengths?

▶ Not if you want your quilt to be square. Nearly all quilt tops are stretched out of shape just a bit after assembly—from all the sewing and handling. The sides probably aren't even the same length. If you cut border strips to match side dimensions and lengths are uneven, your quilt will be skewed forever. It's easy to measure and cut borders that will square up your quilt. You'll be so glad you took the time to do it.

Here is how to assemble the quilt top:

1. Arrange the nine-patch blocks into three diagonal rows of three blocks, placing them on point with the medium dark (C) fabric squares pointing up and down. Place the four Snowball blocks on point between them.
2. Use the pieced setting triangles to fill in the gaps around the quilt's top, bottom, and sides.

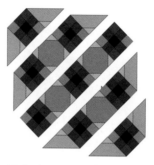

Fig. 15-9 **Arranging the quilt components**

3. Sew the components of each diagonal row together, matching edges and seams carefully. Press seams toward the Snowball blocks
4. Sew the rows together, matching seams carefully. Press new seams in either direction.
5. Square up one end of the 7¼" × 15" medium light strip reserved for corner triangles, then cut two 7¼" × 7¼" squares from it. Cut each square in half once diagonally to make two corner triangles. The fabric's straight grain runs parallel to the short edges of the triangle.

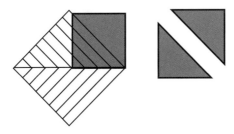

Fig. 15-10 **Cut the corner triangles**

6. Fold a corner triangle in half and finger crease to find the center of its longest edge. Match the crease to the mid-point of a nine-patch, dark square corner of the quilt, right sides together. Sew the corner triangle to the quilt. Press the seam allowance toward the corner triangle.

7. Use the same technique to sew the remaining three corner triangles to the quilt top.

Sew on Borders and Finish the Quilt

The borders of a quilt serve the same purpose as a picture frame—they enhance and highlight the piece they surround. I like to sew on multiple borders, and often use a very dark fabric first to highlight the quilt top, followed by one or more wider borders. You use the borders to repeat fabrics in the quilt, or choose something entirely different.

Adding borders to the quilt gives you the opportunity to square up small inconsistencies in its dimensions, but you'll have to use a specific method to do that. Before you begin, read the instructions for measuring and sewing butted borders in Chapter 4. Press all seam allowances toward the borders.

ELSEWHERE ON THE WEB

▶ Border print fabrics are designed with multiple, decorative stripes of different widths that run along the fabric's lengthwise grain. They make stunning borders or sashing for your quilt. Some quilters cut border prints into identical pieces with angled edges, then sew them together to create kaleidoscopic blocks and border intersections. Jinny Beyer (www.jinnybeyer.com) is a famous quilter who designs fabrics for RJR Textiles, including lots of colorful border prints.

Here is how to add borders and finish the quilt:

1. Use the instructions in Chapter 4 to measure and cut the inner side borders from your 2" wide very dark strips. Sew them to the quilt as directed.
2. Repeat to measure, cut and sew the top and bottom inner borders to the quilt, extending them to cover the side borders.
3. Use the same method to measure and cut the wide side borders. Cut the side borders from two 7½" x 42" dark strips and sew them to the quilt.
4. Use the remaining three 7½" wide border strips to construct the top and bottom borders. They will be approximately 56" long each. Piece each border from one 7½" x 42" long strip and a portion of the third. Instructions in Chapter 4 explain how to piece long borders.
5. Refer to the instructions in Chapter 9 to finish the quilt. You'll mark the top for quilting if necessary, sandwich it with batting and backing, hand or machine quilt it, then sew mitered binding to the quilt's edges with a ¼" seam. Be sure to add a hanging sleeve so that it's easy to display the quilt on a wall. You'll find hanging sleeve options also in Chapter 9.

Get Linked

You'll find more information about vintage textiles and reproduction fabrics at my About.com Quilting Web site, including photo galleries of new releases from several fabric manufacturers.

QUILTING FABRICS AND EMBELLISHMENTS

An index of articles and galleries about quilting fabric and its care.

http://about.com/quilting/fabricembellishment

COLOR VALUE BASICS

Learn how to compare and sort fabrics from light to dark in order to make some design elements stand out and others recede.

http://about.com/quilting/colorvalue

Appendix A

Glossary

appliqué
    The process of sewing one or more smaller pieces of fabric onto a larger background. Appliqué can be done by hand or by machine.

backing
    The fabric panel used as the back piece of a layered quilt.

backstitch
    Stitching backwards over previous stitches to strengthen seams and keep them from unraveling.

basting
    Temporary stitches that secure layers in preparation for quilting with another finishing process; safety pins are used to baste machine-quilted quilts.

batting
    The material used as a stuffing between the quilt top and quilt backing.

bearding
    Batting fibers migrating through a quilt's top or backing and sticking to the outer surface of fabric.

betweens
    Short, sturdy needles used to hand quilt.

bias
    Fabric cuts made at a 45-degree angle to the straight grain. Quilters call any cut that doesn't run parallel to a straight grain a bias cut.

binding
    Cloth that covers and protects the outer edges of the quilt sandwich.

bleeding
    The loss of dyes in a fabric when it gets wet; dyes can stain other fabrics.

chain piecing
    An assembly-line sewing method where components are fed through the sewing machine one after another without breaking the threads between them.

colorfast
    Threads and fabrics that do not fade excessively or bleed when wet.

color value
    How dark or light a color appears to be when compared to other colors.

concave curve
    A curve that rounds inward, like a bite out of a cookie.

convex curve
    A curve that rounds outward.

crocking
    Excess dye particles rubbing off of a dry fabric onto another dry fabric.

crosswise grain
    Threads that run perpendicular to the fabric's selvage; also called weft threads.

design wall
    Any wall where you can position quilting components and then step back to view the layout at a distance. White flannel can be used to make a quick design wall.

directional print
    A fabric printed with a design that has an obvious direction to it, such as a stripe.

easing
    The act of pinning components and using your fingers to adjust adjoining units of uneven lengths so they match for sewing. This is also called easing in.

fabric grain
    The arrangement of threads in fabric.

fat eighth
    One-eighth yard of fabric that is usually cut to measure 9" x 22" rather than the typical one-eighth yard cut of 4.5" x 44".

fat quarter
    One-fourth yard of fabric that usually measures 18" x 22" instead of the typical 9" x 44" quarter-yard cut.

feed dogs
    Metal teeth on a sewing machine that emerge from a hole in the throat plate to grip the underneath of the fabric and help advance it under the needle.

finished size
    The size of a block, patch, or other component in a quilt after all adjacent units are sewn to it.

foundation template
    A full-sized copy of an entire or portion of a quilt; fabric is sewn onto the foundation template.

Hera marker
    A hand tool with a sharp edge that can be used to make creases in fabric.

in the ditch
    Quilting stitches that are sewn close to and parallel to seams.

lengthwise grain
    Threads that run parallel to the fabric's selvage edges; also called warp threads.

loft
    Indicates height. In quilting, loft describes the thickness of batting; it is also used to describe the slight rise in height along seams where seam allowances are pressed underneath them.

meander quilting
    Random quilting stitches that move across the quilt in a gentle motion; stitches do not overlap.

needleturn appliqué
    A type of hand appliqué where edges of shapes are turned under with the tip of the needle as they are sewn to the background.

on point
    A quilt layout where quilt blocks are arranged with their corners pointing up and down to create a series of diagonal rows.

outline quilting
    Hand or machine quilting that outlines a shape in order to emphasize it.

patchwork
    A fabric ensemble created when individual pieces of fabric are sewn together to create a design.

quilt sandwich

The three layers of a quilt that have been prepared for quilting: the quilt top, the inner quilt batting, and the rear backing.

rotary cutter

A cutting device with a round blade, similar to a pizza cutter but razor sharp.

selvage

A tightly woven edge that runs along both outermost edges of a fabric's lengthwise grain.

setting triangles

Triangles used to fill in the jagged edges around outer edges of a quilt with blocks arranged on point.

sharps

Long, thin needles used for hand appliqué and other types of hand sewing.

stipple quilting

Closely spaced, random quilting stitches that flatten the quilted area; stitches are similar to meander quilting but are closer together.

strip set

Multiple fabrics that are sewn together to create a composite unit that can be cut apart to yield smaller pre-sewn segments, eliminating the handling of individual pieces of fabric.

subcut

The act of cutting shorter segments from a long strip of fabric you have prepared for patchwork shapes; also refers to the segments cut from a strip pieced unit.

throat plate

The metal plate beneath a sewing machine's needle and presser foot. The throat plate has openings for the needle and for feed dogs.

UFO

An unfinished object, quilts that we start but never finish.

whole cloth

A quilt made from a single type of fabric, often white, but can be any color or print; embellishment relies on quilting stitches.

Appendix B

Other Sites and Further Readings

Other Sites

Alliance for American Quilts

A nonprofit company dedicated to documenting and preserving American quilts and the stories of their makers, vintage and contemporary.

www.quiltalliance.org/index.html

The Appliqué Society

An organization devoted to furthering the art of appliqué. Attend the annual shows and join a local chapter to increase your knowledge of the technique.

www.theAppliquesociety.org/index.htm

C&T Publishing

C&T publishes a large line of quilting, craft, and other textile-related books.

www.ctpub.com/

Free Quilt Care Course

This free course arrives in your e-mail in eight lessons and was developed by Nancy Kirk of the Kirk Collection, an expert on textile history and care.

www.kirkcollection.com/quiltcarecourse.html

Martingale & Company

Martingale & Company publishes quilting, craft, and other fiber arts books. The company also offers several specialty tools for quilters. You might know the company by one of its imprints: That Patchwork Place.

www.martingale-pub.com/

Marcus Brothers Textiles

Marcus Brothers produces a large number of quilting fabrics from several designers, including lots of reproduction fabrics from past eras.

www.marcusbrothers.com

Museum of the American Quilter's Society

Located in Paducah, Kentucky, the MAQS is open year around. The museum houses permanent and temporary quilt exhibits and features challenges and contests that you can learn about online.

www.quiltmuseum.org

Printing on Fabric

Hewlett Packard offers a complete Web site devoted to using your home printer to print on fabric.

www.shopping.hp.com click on "Activity Center" under "Learn, Use & Create," then click on "Quilting"

Quilt as You Go Stained Glass Appliqué

Quilter's Newsletter Magazine shows you how to create an easy stained glass quilt.
http://qnm.com/articles/feature26/index3.html

RJR Fabrics Free Patterns

An online library of free quilting patterns from a popular fabric manufacturer.
www.rjrfabrics.com click on "Quilt Designs" then "Free Patterns."

Robert Kaufman Fabrics Free Patterns

Robert Kaufman Fabrics is another manufacturer that provides a large library of free quilting patterns on its Web site.
www.robertkaufman.com/quilting/quilts_patterns

Thread Theory

An easy to understand article that explains how to choose threads and needles.
www.quiltbus.com/threadtheory.htm

Further Reading

The American Quilt by Roderick Kiracofe with Mary Elizabeth Johnson

The book's subtitle, a History of Cloth and Comfort, 1750 – 1950, offers a brief preview of what you'll find inside this book. It's filled with color photos of antique quilts, along with thorough explanations of their origins and folklore associated with them. A must have for quilt history buffs.

Baltimore Beauties and Beyond: Studies in Classic Album Quilt Appliqué by Elly Sienkiewicz

A step-by-step approach to creating a quilt reminiscent of the Baltimore Album quilts that were so popular in the mid-1800s.

Heirloom Machine Quilting by Harriet Hargrave

Currently in its fourth edition, this book just keeps getting better and better. The book is packed with all the techniques you need to learn machine quilting.

Machine Quilting Made Easy by Maurine Noble

Machine quilting basics tucked into a relatively small, inexpensive book. The book is an excellent primer for anyone who wants to learn machine quilting.

The New Appliqué Sampler: Learn To Appliqué The Piece O' Cake Way by Becky Goldsmith and Linda Jenkins

Part of the Piece O' Cake series, this edition helps you learn many different types of appliqué and offers quilt patterns to get you started.

Poakalani: Hawaiian Quilts Volume II by Poakalani and John Serrao

A good beginner's guide to Hawaiian appliqué, with complete instructions and patterns that are intricate without overwhelming a new quilter.

Quick-Strip Paper Piecing: For Blocks, Borders & Quilts by **Peggy Martin**

> Ms. Martin combines strip piecing with foundation paper piecing. Her technique is easy to understand and helps you put your quilts together quickly and accurately.

Quiltmaking by Hand: Simple Stitches, Exquisite Quilts by **Jinny Beyer**

> Jinny Beyer is an award-winning quilter and fabric designer, and she pieces and quilts all of her quilts by hand. She shares her techniques with us in this wonderful book.

Rotary Magic: Easy Techniques to Instantly Improve Every Quilt You Make by **Nancy Johnson-Srebro**

> A rotary cutting primer filled with techniques, cutting charts, and plenty of firsthand advice about mastering the skill.

Templates

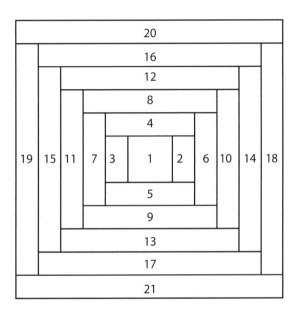

Fig. C-1 Courthouse Steps block

Scan the Courthouse Steps block into your computer at 200 percent, then draw a line ¼" from each edge to represent the outer-most seam allowance. Refer to Chapter 8 for more instructions.

Fig. C-2 **Miscellaneous appliqué templates**

Enlarge as needed for your appliqué projects.

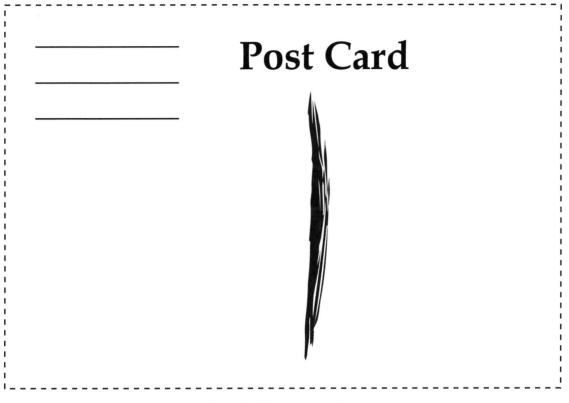

Fig. C-3 **Fabric postcard back**

Scan into your computer at 100 percent and print on fabric for use in your postcards. See Chapter 10 for more information.

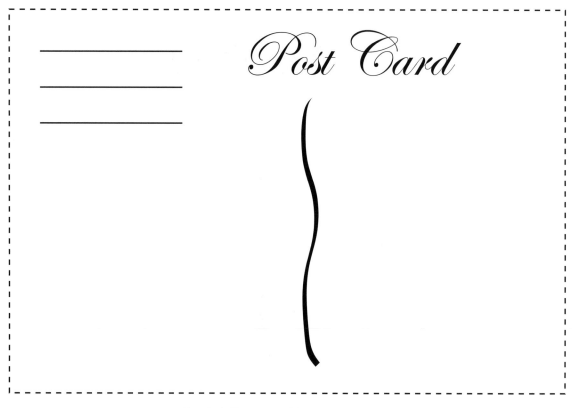

Post Card

Fig. C-4 **One more fabric postcard back**

Scan at 100 percent to equal 4" × 6" each and use as described
on the previous page and in Chapter 10.

Index